The Highly Effective

Books to make you better

Books to make you better. To make you *be* better, *do* better, *feel* better. Whether you want to upgrade your personal skills or change your job, whether you want to improve your managerial style, become a more powerful communicator, or be stimulated and inspired as you work.

Prentice Hall Business is leading the field with a new breed of skills, careers and development books. Books that are a cut above the mainstream – in topic, content and delivery – with an edge and verve that will make you better, with less effort.

Books that are as sharp and as smart as you are.

Prentice Hall Business.
We work harder – so you don't have to.

For more details on products, and to contact us, visit
www.pearsoned.co.uk

The Highly Effective Marketing Plan

Peter Knight

PEARSON
Prentice Hall
BUSINESS

London • New York • Toronto • Sydney • Tokyo • Singapore
Hong Kong • Cape Town • Madrid • Paris • Amsterdam • Munich • Milan

PEARSON EDUCATION LIMITED

Edinburgh Gate
Harlow CM20 2JE
Tel: +44 (0)1279 623623
Fax: +44 (0)1279 431059
Website: www.pearson-books.com

First published in Great Britain in 2004

ISBN 0 273 687867

British Library Cataloguing in Publication Data
A CIP catalogue record for this book can be obtained from the British Library

Library of Congress Cataloging-in-Publication Data
A catalogue record for this book is available from the Library of Congress

10 9 8 7 6 5 4 3 2
08 07 06 05 04

Typeset by 70
Printed and bound in Great Britain by Bell & Bain Ltd, Glasgow

The Publishers' policy is to use paper manufactured from sustainable forests.

Contents

This book is dedicated to Gill & Tony Tugman

Acknowledgements

Do **people read these?** I'm scared stiff of missing people out and causing great offence, so instead please accept these catch-alls – you know how much you've helped me.

HEMP wouldn't have happened without:

- everyone at Pearson
- everyone at Phoenix, and particularly Sophie, Paul, Clare and Vikki
- many clients current and past, and particularly Redcup
- lots of suppliers and business contacts
- my business coaches, trainers and mentors
- TEC International
- my friends
- my family, and particularly Debbie and Chessie
- and especially my mum – yeah, I know – the person I want to single out for so much going way beyond the call of duty

About this book – how to get what you want from it

This book has five elements. There's the full version of HEMP, divided into fifteen chapters. As some of these will be more relevant to some readers than others, there's a synopsis of each chapter as well. It's quite alright to skip things which others might need to learn or relearn. A single case study of Redcup, a real company who created a very successful HEMP, is contained within each chapter. And there's "HEMP in Action" – examples of brilliant communications to help inspire you. At the end of the book you'll find HEMP lessons which reveal things several companies discovered about themselves following completing their HEMP. Their examples should be motivating for many businesses.

What is HEMP?

A **Highly Effective Marketing Plan (HEMP)** is a process that will dramatically improve your chances of profitably selling more of your products and services. And HEMP will stop you wasting thousands, maybe millions, of pounds, dollars, euros or yen on marketing initiatives that should never see the light of day.

HEMP is a straightforward, simple, fifteen-step plan which you can use to address your problems and opportunities whatever their size, whatever your business, and whatever the sector in which you operate.

A HEMP is immediately understood by colleagues, partners, team members, financiers and anyone else involved with your project. It gets straight to the "meat and potato" and helps you communicate your exciting opportunity in a way that engages people so they want to be involved. And it's tried, tested and proven. Hundreds of companies of all shapes and sizes use HEMP. Read what some of them have to say about it:

"A very refreshing and simple yet focused approach to develop a marketing plan!" Stephen Bean, Commercial Director

Guardian IT

"Clear, concise and informative – focused on the key issues, avoiding all the jargon!" Patrick Stirland, Managing Director

The Mitie Group

"Helped me to see a path through the muddy confused waters of marketing; another tool for the busy marketer."

Steve Hazell, Marketing Director

Snow & Rock Sports Ltd

"Peter Knight's insight into the marketing process and his energetic and practical method of ensuring a plan is well drawn out and easy to use gets as close to a guaranteed outcome as I have come across in a long time. If you are looking for 'True North' and want a way of getting there read and implement HEMP."

Bob Battye

Group Chair for TEC

"Forests have been unnecessarily sacrificed to trying to put across the best way to develop an effective marketing plan. Most of the books written serve only to make a basically simple process seem a form of black magic. Peter Knight brings a process and clarity of thought to this area which is startling both in its simplicity and effectiveness. I hugely recommend HEMP as essential reading for anyone involved in or interested by Marketing."

Chris Hughes

TEC Chair

"HEMP has proven an invaluable tool in the development and implementation of the First Choice mainstream brands' tactical marketing and communications activity. As well as the creative work that Phoenix has produced, HEMP appears to be a simple yet effective way of planning any company's marketing communications."

Rachel Clayton Head of Marketing

First Choice Holidays & Flights

"Excellent, well worthwhile." Ian Moore, Marketing Manager
The Commtech Group Plc

"Inspiring, informative and thought provoking. Highly recommended." Emma Soames, Marketing & Communications Co-ordinator
Verbatim

"This is something that every senior executive should consider if they are truly committed to effective planning."
Gina Collman, Head of Corporate Communications
GMAC RFC – A General Motors Company

"Clearly focused strategy for addressing specific issues."
Ariane Wilkinson, Marketing Director
Cyber Source International Ltd

"Will be of good use in the future business. I would happily recommend it." Jamie Prentice, General Sales Manager
HWM Audi

"Thought provoking, challenging and stimulating."
Hilary Khoo, Director
Khoo Systems Ltd

"HEMP will certainly aid my marketing strategy and plan for 2002." Clare Murdoch, Business Development Manager
Parkeray Ltd

"Eloquently and admirably guides 'lay-marketeers' through a minefield of strategy which makes valuable sense."

Jacqui Cox, PR & Marketing Consultant
Barker Interiors

"Highly motivational and practical which will be of great benefit to future company strategy and strategic thinking."

Ivan Thompson, Managing Director

R S Stokvis & Sons Ltd

"A fantastic simplistic approach that takes you back to the basics and really makes you think about where you are going with that marketing plan." Clare Stevens, Business Manager

Influence at Work (UK) Ltd

"Up there with the best in marketing. A refreshingly new approach to marketing planning that will be invaluable to all marketers. Set to become a classic."

Michael R Jones, Managing Director

Cairnforth Ltd

Setting the scene – Why do you need a HEMP?

You've got a product or service that you want to tell people about, in the most effective way, at the lowest cost. So you need a marketing plan.

Beware before you begin: there's almost as much bullshit as waste in marketing. Waste just edges it though.

Think about it. How many times today will somebody try to get your attention for their product or service which you don't want, need or care about? Or look at it another way, how many advertisements, mail shots, phone calls or emails have caused you to buy something today? Or this week? Or this month?

On the other hand, the world has many examples of excess. How much stuff have you got that is wasteful, unnecessary, unused or forgotten? As so many people repeatedly buy stuff they don't need, or even want, is it any wonder that advertisers continue their scattergun, "throw enough crap against the wall, some of it must stick" approach?

Despite the fact that wasteful practices are bad news for your business, and for the world, nothing seems to change. This, I believe, is fundamentally down to tradition, waste's favourite bed partner. "We've always done it this way" is a familiar mantra and even when realising the absurdity of continuing practices which should be long confined to history, many companies still do what they've always done but just dress things up a bit differently, put new packaging on a tired old product, run a new-look campaign in the belief this will re-inject a new life force (and it's this that fuels waste).

'We've always done it this way' is a familiar mantra

Those of you who are new to marketing or have relied on others to provide this function would be totally disbelieving of some of the practices repeated daily.

Marketing has developed words, expressions and jargon which is even more difficult to decipher and yet, frighteningly, no-one seems to question it. Worse, they adopt it themselves. I'm convinced there's a small group of (highly influential) people out there who dream up new words every day and plant them within marketing circles to see how long it takes for their adoption. And this language is more harmful than any computer virus I've seen, as it affects the hard drives of previously sane people – sometimes permanently.

Marketing Bingo is a game we sometimes play when meeting clients who are prone to using marketing jargon. There are ten words or phrases on a card to be listened for, then discreetly ticked off, and the winner is the first with a complete set who manages to engineer "Bingo" into the conversation.

I knew that even this distraction wouldn't help me in a meeting with one marketing director who actually said, "Our endgame solution lies in synergising our channels thereby upping the priority to ensure brand sanitation when populating our presentation collateral."

This was the moment I knew HEMP was needed – a Highly Effective Marketing Plan free of all the language that so many self-styled professionals use to disguise their way into clients' wallets. A process which filters out all the bullshit and gets to the real issues with sparkling clarity, thereby ensuring waste is exterminated, and profits improved or created.

Who's going to get their highs from HEMP?

If you're in business, or are planning to be, you need a HEMP. If you're a Chief Executive or this is your very first job then a HEMP is for you too. And whether your business is global or your entire world is contained within a 500-yard radius, a HEMP is just as applicable.

To create a HEMP you don't need to be in marketing or have any marketing background or qualifications, although if you have them a HEMP will add to your skills. (Actually it will probably make redundant several other processes you currently use.) Marketing isn't something exclusively for the marketing department, it impacts on every area of the business. Indeed, in the words of Jeff Faulkner, former managing director of Barratt Homes, when I was promoted to marketing director, "Peter, marketing is too important to leave to the marketing director!" And he's right. Whether you're aware of it or not, your marketing plan is the driver of your business, even if it's never been written and is lurking in a dark corner of your grey matter. You might not call it a marketing plan, or indeed dislike the idea of marketing in any form (with so much bullshit around this isn't surprising), but it's what makes your business grow or die. And therefore everyone needs a HEMP.

 Your marketing plan is the driver of your business ""

HEMP – a real example

Theory is all well and good, and let's face it there are lots of books about marketing theory. A HEMP is a real process, and it works. So, to bring it to life, you're going to see a HEMP being created. And at the same time you can create your own if you choose.

I'm grateful to the directors of Redcup, who created a HEMP when they started their company less than two years ago, for allowing me to use their experience, and success, as a real case study. The Redcup story will show you how, by creating a HEMP, their whole strategy and marketing communications were changed from those they were originally thinking of using. Indeed, they attribute a large amount of their success to having a HEMP:

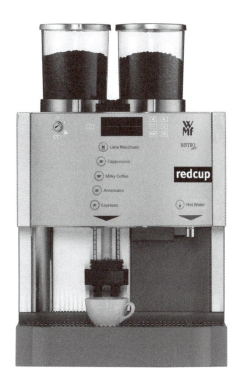

There is no way Redcup would have achieved such meteoric success without our creating a HEMP

Richard Bright, Chairman

Redcup

How to get the most from this book

People like to work differently and I've learned not to be prescriptive with a "one size fits all" approach. So you might like to create your first HEMP whilst reading this book, or you might prefer to read the book from cover to cover and then begin – it's your choice. A pen, a single piece of A4 paper and a couple of hours or so of your time is all you need to get started.

HEMP is a sequential process and therefore you should read this book in order if you're creating your HEMP as you go (otherwise feel free to leap around all over the place). I'm indebted to Julian Ranger, the managing director of Staysys, the highly technical software company that supplies the defence industry, who suggested that for some people HEMP works even better as a "map", or as one of the great teachers of this world; Colin Blundell, calls it, a "Spidergram".

If you would like to visit **www.phoenixplc.com/hemp** you can download a HEMP template of your choice.

So are you ready for a HEMP?
Let's get started.

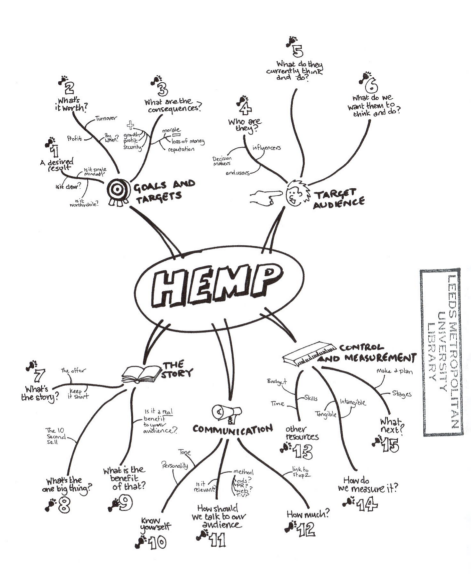

The chapters in brief

The first step in creating your HEMP is to get as clear as possible in your mind, and then written down on a piece of paper, what you want to achieve – I call this the "desired result". Sounds simple doesn't it, and to be blunt, bloody obvious too. However, experience shows me that many people don't do this – they go off and start spending their own or their company's money without really knowing what they're hoping to achieve.

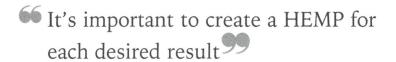 It's important to create a HEMP for each desired result

It's important to create a HEMP for each desired result (if you have several that is). This chapter emphasises how you'll end up with an IMP (Ineffective Marketing Plan) if you try this proven process with more than one desired result.

Step one gives you some ideas to think about and questions to answer to enable you to clarify and get really specific with your desired result. Also, by writing and then refining your desired result, you'll have something which you can easily communicate to all the other people from whom you're going to need to get buy-in, whether this be your boss, your colleagues or your bank manager.

So here are the three main points of step one:

1. It must be something worthwhile – for you

2. It must be a single desired result

3. It must have great clarity and be very easily understood

HEMP STEP 2 – What's it worth?

If you're going to do something, then value it. And identifying a monetary value helps create a universal currency, as others might view differently the worth you attach to your project.

I know it's not always about money. Sometimes there are other reasons for doing things which are more important, but in step two you'll find a way of calculating the financial value as well. This is because other people might not be as motivated by your big idea as you are, but they will be turned on by how much it's worth.

By properly calculating the value of your desired result it will set the framework for the rest of your plan, not least in later steps where you'll identify the investment and resources you need to achieve it.

This chapter will reinforce the importance of identifying the turnover and profit, which in itself will greatly aid getting your plan approved, or raising the finance, or both.

HEMP STEP 3 – What are the consequences?

I want you to really think about all the consequences that your plan might have before you start it. Step three will help you identify all the upsides, not just financial, as well as all the other good stuff. Also, you will carefully consider the potential downsides – your plan will almost certainly have some. There's another key piece to this chapter as well – what happens if you don't implement your plan? Rarely do people consider this, and yet, not doing something can be as significant as doing something, or even more so. By working through this step of your HEMP you will discover powerful arguments which you can use to persuade other people to support your initiative. Seeing all the possible consequences once your desired result is achieved allows you to mitigate difficult issues, up front, before they have any impact.

This step is also a very useful check to make sure that your desired result is really worth it. After all, if you discover that there are more problems created than solved you may need to reconsider. On the upside, you may discover even more positive consequences than you first envisaged.

HEMP STEP 4 – Targets

Who are you after? Who will be buying your product or service?

The simple premise underpinning this chapter is that the better you know who you're selling to, the more likely you are to do business with them. And this step encourages you to find ways of really getting to know your target audience(s).

If you identify that you need to communicate with several people – for example both parents, and their children, may need to be persuaded that this year's "must have" is right for them – you may need to create a separate branch for your HEMP at this stage, as an advert appealing to six year olds is going to be different, I imagine, than one for their mothers.

This step is all about really finding out who you're going to be dealing with, and I mean really finding out.

HEMP STEP 5 – What do they currently think and do?

Having completed step four you know who you're after. This chapter highlights how important it is for you to know both what they think, as well as what they currently do.

The principle behind this step (and step six) is that thinking always precedes doing. And if you want to change the doing from, for example, buying a competitor's service to buying yours instead, for example, you need to change the way your targets think. And to do this you need to know what they think now.

This chapter asks questions which will get you to probe into the minds of your customers, to get them, metaphorically, on your couch, and to really learn how to understand them.

HEMP STEP 6 – What do you want them to think and do?

By now you'll have seen that HEMP is a sequential process. This chapter gets you to think about how you would like your customers to think before they do what you want them to do!

As thinking always precedes doing, you need to understand how you want your targets to think about your product and service. One of the reasons for this is that with clever communications you can change the way people think. There is so much wasteful advertising trying to get people to do things differently rather than causing them to think and then do things differently.

HEMP STEP 7 – What's the story?

What are you actually selling? This chapter prompts the exercise of succinctly writing down exactly what's on offer. This exercise is amazing for many people who, whilst believing they know what they do, actually discover that either they don't, or they can't adequately describe it.

This step will help you jettison all the awful jargon which might have crept into your vocabulary. Instead, you will create a motivating and compelling script which beautifully describes your desired result.

HEMP STEP 8 – Your one big thing (AKA the ten-second sell)

All too often people's descriptions of their service, or product, are boring and confusing, filled with far too much irrelevant detail. This chapter gets you to distil down to the **one** big thing on offer.

Part of creating a HEMP is the ability to sum up, in less than ten seconds, in a magnetic way, exactly what it is you do or are going to do.

HEMP STEP 9 – What's the benefit of that?

This chapter helps you to make sure that your one big thing is something that actually benefits your customers – if it doesn't then you need another one big thing.

This step helps you avoid the trap of believing that something like your innovative process or sophisticated IT turns your customer on. It doesn't, what customers love is what your product or service will do for them.

HEMP STEP 10 – Know yourself

Who are you? This step is where you get to find out. Sometimes companies think they have one personality when in reality (of course reality is what the customer thinks) they're something very different. Of course, if you're going to be highly effective then it helps if your business personality really appeals to your clients, so this chapter helps you address this issue.

You'll find some helpful ideas so you can really work out what your company's current personality is, and if necessary, what it should be.

HEMP STEP 11 – How will you talk to your targets?

This chapter highlights many of the different ways you could speak to your targets and proposes which are the most effective in different circumstances. The point is made that no single communication method provides all the answers. Indeed, many are becoming less effective than they used to be, and what can you do about this – other than spend more? When you create your HEMP you can use this section as a guide to check that you've considered all the options.

HEMP STEP 12 – How much?

What's your budget? Compare this with the numbers written down in step two: is it realistic? Compare this with the ideas you've got from step eleven: again, is it realistic? If not, then some rethinking is required.

HEMP STEP 13 – Other resources

This chapter focuses on the other things you'll need, in addition to money, to get your HEMP into action. The key thing here is to identify up front, as much as possible, all the other people, premises, machines, etc, that will need to be utilised. By determining resources in advance, you can carefully plan how you will get others to provide them for you.

Also this step asks you to assess realistically how much of your time will be needed for this HEMP, as for many there's still the existing business to be concerned with. What's going to give? What will you delegate or stop doing so you can focus on your plan?

HEMP STEP 14 – Measure it

How will you know that your HEMP is on track? How will you measure it? Here we explore how important it is to have as many indicators as possible and some of the different mechanisms that will help you in navigating through to your desired result. Many plans fail to do this, but your HEMP will have lots of measurements in place before you start spending any money.

HEMP STEP 15 – What next?

Sometimes even a HEMP can seem daunting, particularly knowing where to start. This chapter helps you to identify the beginning and to map out the first steps.

Making your HEMP come alive

This chapter has tips and ideas to help your HEMP come alive as opposed to sitting in a cupboard waiting for someone else to activate it.

HEMP lessons

At the end of the book are several real examples of companies of varying sizes and from diverse business sectors which have used the HEMP process and achieved amazing results as a consequence. Often the lessons were not expected, and these might spark ideas for you to consider.

HEMP in action   example 1

Throughout the book you will see examples of Highly Effective Marketing which I hope will inspire you to be as imaginative and creative as the people who came up with these ideas. Of course, as creative directors of all advertising agencies will acknowledge, great advertising starts with a detailed and clear brief – which is what a HEMP will also give you.

Some of the ideas required millions to be invested, others very little. To be creative does not necessarily require big budgets, but always requires straightforward intelligence.

The first example of HEMP in action is a campaign created by Leo Burnett, Johannesburg, for its client, Rose Taxis. Notice how relevant the idea is, how it's directed solely to the people who are likely to need the service, at the appropriate time – quite brilliant, and on a tiny budget too.

Client: Rose Taxis
Agency: Lobedu Leo Burnett, Johannesburg, 1998

A DESIRED RESULT

I've seen, and I bet you have too, many people setting out on a new project or initiative with no clear idea of what they're seeking to achieve. Companies often set themselves vague targets such as "growth", "success" or "improvement" without properly defining what these mean. If your company has a goal which states something along the lines of either "World Class", "Best in the Industry", "Market Leader", "No. 1", "Upper Quartile" or some other similar, largely meaningless term, then you need to get much more detailed. Because if you've no idea where you're headed then how will you know when you get there?

"Would you tell me, please, which way I ought to go from here?

"That depends a good deal on where you want to get to", said the cat.

"I don't much care where . . ." said Alice.

"Then it doesn't matter which way you go," said the cat.

Alice's Adventures in Wonderland, Lewis Carroll

It may be that the reason some companies are not specific about their desired result is that they fear employees will achieve it too easily and therefore will not work hard enough. Or, perhaps they feel inadequate about setting a stretching, yet believable, target as so many management books have implanted a belief that only doubling or trebling performance each year is good enough. On the other hand, something that kills off many a plan are those ideas that are just too large, too ambitious; ones that frighten more than they excite.

"I can't believe that!" said Alice.

"Can't you?" the Queen said in a pitying tone. "Try again: draw a long breath, and shut your eyes."

Alice laughed. "There's no use trying" she said. "One can't believe impossible things."

"I dare say you haven't had much practice," said the Queen. "When I was your age, I always did it for half an hour a day. Why, sometimes I've believed as many as six impossible things before breakfast."

Alice Through the Looking Glass, Lewis Carroll

- What do you want to achieve?
- What increase in sales do you want? Over what timescale?
- What new product or service are you seeking to launch?
- What's your big idea? What will it feel like when you achieve it?

These are the sort of questions you need to answer to start your HEMP. It's all about creating a really well formed outcome, where you picture as clearly as possible the specific result your HEMP will achieve. And the greater the clarity the more likely that others will "get it" and buy into your idea.

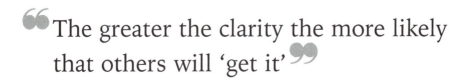

The greater the clarity the more likely that others will 'get it'

Your desired result can be as small or as large as you want it to be, but please make it something that is very worthwhile for you. You could, for example, choose to create a HEMP where the desired result is to open for business in a new country and create sales with a value of £100 million within two years. Alternatively, at the other end of the scale, your HEMP desired result might be to attract one new client for one of your services in just eight weeks.

One of the great things about the HEMP process is how applicable it is to problems and opportunities of all sizes. Indeed, once you have completed your first HEMP, not only will you have a plan to implement, you will also have learned how to create a HEMP for any issue you might have in the future. For example, many people have used HEMP to promote themselves, where their desired result has been to find the "perfect job". I've seen HEMPs for people seeking promotion either for an immediate opportunity or for a role they aspire to achieve within two to three years. Your HEMP can be totally focused on influencing just one person, or several million – the process is the same.

Many HEMPs have the desired result of making more sales, one way or another, and therefore often are focused on an external audience. Your HEMP will be just as effective if your desired result is to get something extra from your team, or some other internal audience. I've seen one UK division of a US parent use HEMP with a desired result of increased investment. (In fact, to be specific, which is very important at this stage of your HEMP, its desired result was to "get those bean counters in Chicago to give us the $10 million we need and to take us more seriously"!)

Your desired result can be an expansion or improvement in your existing business or to launch something brand new. As you will know, it tends to be harder to launch a new product or service and it's harder still when you're introducing something brand new to a totally new audience. The good news is that by creating a HEMP you will ask yourself all the key questions, which when answered will substantially increase your odds of obtaining that desired result – yes, even that tricky one!

In every case, like so many other things in life, it's the start point that matters most. Your whole HEMP will be shaped by your desired result and if, whilst completing the process, things don't feel quite as they should, then return here and have another look at your objective. It may need expanding or contracting or usually just greater clarity.

66Your whole HEMP will be shaped by your desired result99

Often the main objective gets lost as it gets surrounded by peripheral stuff or unnecessary detail. As you will see from the Redcup example below, there is no ambiguity here, no confusion, just the desired result expressed in a language anyone can understand.

Example Redcup

Redcup is a brand new start-up company which plans to supply very high quality beverages, primarily coffee, to offices. The desired result for Redcup is to be the beverage supplier to 5,000 clients within twelve months.

Your desired result should succinctly state what you will do, and by when. No more at this stage (there are steps later on within your HEMP when you can add more detail).

Some people are tempted to try and create a HEMP with two or more desired results. This doesn't work. Instead create a separate HEMP for each desired result, even if they are quite similar. There's nothing stopping you combining things later, but at this stage it's really important to get as focused as possible as, after all, we're going to create a Highly Effective Marketing Plan, not a general catch-all marketing plan – aren't we?

HEMP STEP 1 Key points

The three most important things you should consider when forming your desired result are:

● It must be something worthwhile – for you

● It must be a single desired result

● It must have great clarity and be very easily understood

Proceed to step two once you've created a desired result in your mind, and written it down.

HEMP in action   example 2

First Choice, the leading UK holiday company, was launching a new brochure to promote its competitively priced holidays under its Sunquest brand. As you can no doubt imagine, travel agents receive hundreds of brochures, so to make the Sunquest brochure stand out it was accompanied by a bar of chocolate which was decorated in Sunquest's livery. The recipients, front counter travel agents, are young women aged between 18 and 25 who typically consume a lot of chocolate! The result was that the travel agents were so appreciative of this gift that Sunquest sales exceeded target by 64%. Even if these people were reading other brochures from Sunquest's competitors they were actually digesting the Sunquest message! This is another example of a highly effective, carefully targeted, marketing initiative that came from a HEMP.

Client: Sunquest
Agency: Phoenix

WHAT'S IT WORTH?

Having clearly defined the outcome you wish to achieve, your desired result, take a moment to calculate what it's worth. If you can't or won't put a value on it then your HEMP is going to struggle to come alive. Everything has a value and it's possible in nearly every case to establish what this is. It doesn't necessarily have to be financial, although if your desired result can be measured this way as well then I urge you to consider attaching some numbers.

For example, let's imagine a desired result of recruiting ten new sales people within six months. What is the extra turnover and profit these extra sales people will realistically be expected to achieve within the first year (or other time period if you prefer)? This is important because, to be a highly effective plan, we will want to make sure that any investment (step twelve) and the cost of other resources (step thirteen), is more than covered by the return.

I watched a HEMP successfully unfold where the desired result was to have a new, important piece of equipment allocated and installed in a hospital within twelve months. In the end, the key turning point for securing the additional funding necessary was the very well-considered financial enhancements this machine would achieve. (I suppose the powers-that-be at the NHS have heard just about every possible "life saving" story and are immune to them.) I don't like to consider the outcome had the financial value not been determined.

I met Sharon Jones at a meeting of several "not for profit" organisations in the West Midlands where I was the guest speaker and decided to run a HEMP workshop. Sharon's charity, in simple terms, encourages and helps men to become better fathers. How do you put a financial value on that you might ask? Well, the thing with Sharon's work that struck me so profoundly was the openness and honesty with which she answered this question. Apparently, in poorer UK communities, particularly those with a high proportion of black people, single parent families are the norm. And by single parent we're talking living with mum – as many as 70% of fathers have no contact at all with their children. This has become an accepted way of life, "that's how it is". The cost to society is scary, not least as these children will be parents themselves one day and the negative spiral is likely to continue. Sharon established that by just influencing one father to provide some sort of role model for his children a future possible saving of £100,000 may be achieved (assuming a positive influence would keep a child on the straight and narrow).

Okay, so you've now got a figure in mind. So ask yourself if this is realistic. Are you expecting too much too soon? Or conversely are you being pessimistic? (You know how you tend to be one way or the other.) It's so easy with marketing plans to get carried away with enthusiasm and often the direct consequence is scepticism from those who have heard too much bullshit in the past. Much better to create a compelling plan that builds, in smaller incremental and realistic steps, than one which promises world domination before bedtime.

Are you being honest about the competition and how much market share you can realistically take from them? They may be very poor and what you're planning to offer might be in a different league, however people don't break away from what they're used to easily. Marketing can be very much like building a fire: even with a paraffin-soaked fire-lighter it takes a few minutes for the kindling to catch before you can put the coal or logs on, and then it takes a while before the warmth comes through into the room. Your new product and service is likely to take time to catch on, and you should consider this when projecting the value.

❝Marketing can be very much like building a fire❞

I've heard many times marketing people say they have no competition for their product or service. Bullshit alert! It's statements like these that give marketing such a bad reputation. There's competition for everything. Even if you're planning a brand new, unique, never been seen before product or service, you will still have competition. If you don't believe me ask yourself this question: what are people currently spending their money on which, instead, they will use to buy what you're selling?

How long will it take you to get established? Most new businesses and ventures take longer than expected, often because of the time that's wasted dealing with all the bureaucracy and red tape. Even in larger, long-established companies things can take a while to get going, again largely because of the bureaucracy and red tape (of the company's own design, as opposed to that of government). Will this affect how much you will turn over in year one, and therefore cause you to consider highlighting how your idea will grow in value over a longer period? You might like to run several financial models and select the one that is both motivating and realistically achievable, in other words, *believable*.

As well as the turnover or income your idea will generate, establish how much profit will also be made. It amazes me how often people don't think beyond turnover and yet the purpose of all enterprise is surely to profit from it? Again, be realistic. Your existing product line might achieve a very good profit margin, but then it's been running for several years now and substantial waste has been eliminated. Will the same be true of your new venture? Will you need to price your new service competitively to cause people to change their habits and sample what you're offering before committing to it?

What about contingencies? The jury is out on this one I know, with some believing that the inclusion of a contingency just encourages it to be used. But come on, have you ever had an idea that has run exactly to plan? Even with a HEMP things will change – and change normally costs money. Have you allowed enough?

"Don't wring every last penny out of your idea before it's started, leave some for later"

People react much more favourably to a proposition when they see that someone has "run the numbers". Indeed, a pretty good rule of thumb that a plan has not been well conceived and properly thought through is a lack of detailed financial analysis or generalisation such as "could double our turnover". I urge you to be conservative with your projections. If the investor/bank/accountant/boss can see extra possibilities for profit improvement then you're almost home and dry. Don't wring every last penny out of your idea before it's started, leave some for later.

In most organisations there is competition for a finite budget and limited resources. The common approach is to make ever bigger claims about your venture in the hope that it will stand out and win the day. Often though the opposite is true as the bigger you make it appear the more risk comes along as part of the package. In order for your HEMP to get off the ground make sure that the numbers appeal and add up, that they have room for further improvement and are ambitious, but above all, are realistic and believable.

Example Redcup

Redcup treats every employee as a client, so 5,000 clients spending £5 a week on coffee and other beverages equals £1,300,000.

Redcup works on a 40% gross margin, (prior to overheads, interest and tax) which means that its profit will be £520,000.

HEMP STEP 2 Key points

- Work out what your desired result (step one) is worth

- Make sure you identify the profit or contribution as well as the turnover

- Depending on the time-scale for your desired result you may like to identify the value in the short, medium and longer term

HEMP in action   example 3

The International Childcare Trust (ICT) is a UK registered charity with projects in Africa and Asia that help give some of the world's most deprived children a better start in life. ICT organised a fund-raising event involving cycling across Sri Lanka, coast to coast, to visit two of their centres. I decided to get involved and actually take part as well as promote the event. We needed to find another 20 individuals who were prepared to undertake the equivalent of cycling from London to Brighton every day for a week, across hilly terrain, on jeep and dirt tracks, in the heat of a tropical island, who could also raise several thousand pounds each in sponsorship! But we had no budget: ICT is quite rightly very proud that over 90% of the donations received go directly to the projects. As a consequence, ICT has very little funding available for advertising and promotion. Although we donated our time for free, the largest cost of advertising is the media space. So, we produced these advertisements and sent them to a number of national newspapers asking if they would run them free of charge when space allowed. Also, we produced, in-house, posters which were mailed to every gym, cycling club and sports centre in the UK asking if they could be displayed free of charge, along with a web address **www.cyclesrilanka.com** and various PR activities.

Within a few months, the team was assembled and over £75,000 was raised – considerably more than the highest target initially set. ICT is so pleased with the results that Cycle Sri Lanka will be repeated in 2004 and may even become an annual event.

The ideas and initiatives for ICT's Cycle Sri Lanka started with a HEMP, as its Programmes Co-ordinator, Margaret O'Grady, confirms, *"HEMP actually helped save many children's lives – I can think of no finer endorsement to give."*

To help this child escape poverty we need you to start a revolution.

(actually 711,345 revolutions would be better)

That's how many times the wheel of your bike will need to turn to get you across Sri Lanka as you raise money for children in desperate need of your help.

See our website for more details or call 0845 3300 533

cyclesrilanka.com

international **childcare** trust

UK Charity Commission Registered No. 326240
© International Childcare Trust 2003

Client: International Childcare Trust
Agency: Phoenix

WHAT ARE THE CONSEQUENCES?

Once your plan starts to be implemented it will have consequences. And these are potentially both positive and negative. Try asking the production director of a busy factory how he feels about the new plan to double the sales of the most difficult to construct product the company makes, which has the highest amount of rejects, within three months. The enthusiasm might not be shared!

Many people only look at the upside of their plan and don't consider the possible negative impact. This is why so many marketing plans fail at the first signs of anything going wrong, or even just deviating from the original projection.

Let's look at the positives first. You've already established a realistic value for your desired result, so you know the financial upside. What else are you going to get? It might be that your plan will galvanise a dispirited sales team, or be the catalyst for customers to see your company and its other products in a new light. If you're moving into a new territory for the first time your HEMP may give you glimpses of other markets you could enter next. One client of mine told me how his company received unsolicited approaches from some of its competitor's employees as a consequence of the innovation that came from its HEMP. Another found that trade journalists were not only interested in the idea itself, they also wanted to learn more about the clients other plans and the resultant magazine articles caused a huge rise in profile, something most of us would like.

"Your HEMP may give you glimpses of other markets you could enter next"

The more positive consequences you discover at the planning stage, the more likely your plan will gain the approval often needed. Sure, it has to stack up financially, but often people are at least as motivated by other factors – make sure your HEMP includes these.

The downsides need to be considered just as carefully, not least as this will demonstrate how thoroughly thought out your HEMP is – and thereby dramatically improves its likelihood of implementation. It may be that your initiative will have a significant call on existing resources and whilst this might appear to be a barrier it could also be the "extra" justification needed for that investment. I know of one company that took the long overdue decision to upgrade its IT as a consequence of a HEMP for a new initiative. This initially perceived downside was quickly turned into a huge positive, one much appreciated by the whole company. It really is worthwhile considering, as best as one is able to at this time, just what might go wrong. A common issue is the distraction from the core business and the fear that whilst the new idea will succeed, the price might be a decline in business overall. If this is a very real possibility then flag it up – and find possible solutions while you're at it.

Something that I'd rarely seen before when creating a HEMP was an analysis of what would happen if the plan wasn't implemented. This might seem strange at first but imagine, for example, the impact of not doing something new only to find a few months later that a competitor does exactly what you'd thought of. Also, companies rarely stand still. They tend to either grow or contract, to rise up the industry league table or get relegated. Your plan will cause things to happen, and so other stuff will occur if your plan isn't implemented. Consider the consequence of this.

I've found that often people are more motivated by the fear of loss than they are by the pleasure of gain. This might not be immediately apparent so try these exercises:

Exercise 1

Choose either A or B.

A You can have a guaranteed win of £3,000;

or

B You can have an 80% chance of winning £4,000 and a 20% chance of winning nothing.

Now try:

Exercise 2

Choose either A or B.

A You can have a guaranteed loss of £3,000;

or

B You can have an 80% chance of losing £4,000 and a 20% chance of losing nothing.

Many of us chose A in exercise one and B in exercise two and yet mathematically they are identical and indeed B in both cases offers a better bet statistically.

When dealing with Financial Directors it's often useful to put your case on the basis of what the company might lose if you don't implement your plan. (They've heard a hundred times before enthusiastic claims and are immune to them.) Also, it's further evidence that your plan has been thought through carefully and will be highly effective.

You might like to consider returning to this step once you've completed the rest of the plan as it may need to be refined as a consequence. Often I've seen people scale down or break their desired result into chunks, so creating a greater chance of getting "first round" funding and resources. This is not meant to discourage you from worldwide domination, but it might be best to start locally and build on the success in ever greater increments. Many years ago I used to work for Barratt Homes, the house builder. Sir Lawrie Barratt started his company by building one home for his family, having identified that this was cheaper than buying an existing property he couldn't afford. Fifteen years or so later he was Britain's biggest builder of new homes.

List out separately the upsides and downsides of your HEMP and include what might happen if you don't implement it.

Example **Redcup**

Positives	Negatives
Growth	Lose money
Profit	Let team down
Security	Reputation of failure
Prove the concept –	Missed opportunity
raise funding for expansion	

Redcup opened for business in January 2002 as the coffee revolution was taking hold in the UK. People were choosing to spend £1.75 for a tall skinny latte at Starbucks or Café Nero and clearly the opportunity to sell a machine for the office which would dispense coffee of a similar quality was significant. The Redcup Directors resigned from their jobs within one of the world's leading vending companies and tempted other colleagues to join them in the venture. The upsides were exciting, as everyone could see the potential. However, the downsides with personal guarantees to the bank, initial capital investment and loss of salary and benefits were not insignificant. But the biggest consequence of not achieving the desired result would be the sense of frustration of having missed an opportunity and also the loss of credibility that would have resulted. Indeed, the whole confidence of the individuals might have been irreparably damaged were their HEMP to have just remained on a piece of paper.

> 66 The biggest consequence of not achieving the desired result would be the sense of frustration at having missed an opportunity 99

HEMP STEP 3 Key points

- Identify the upsides and possible downsides of your HEMP

- Spell out what might happen if you don't pursue your desired result, (i.e. do nothing)

- Be realistic and honest – it will help persuade doubters that you've considered all the consequences

HEMP in action   example 4

Direct mail is often referred to as "junk mail" as a consequence of it being so poorly targeted that it's often indirect or misdirected. There are exceptions of course, such as this simple idea for the AA. The mailing was only sent to former AA members who hadn't renewed their membership. Each piece of cardboard inside stated the exact town in which the recipient lived. A perfect example of accurate targeting combined with a powerful and easily understood message. The most effective communications are those which talk to people at the exact moment they might need the product or service, as this one does.

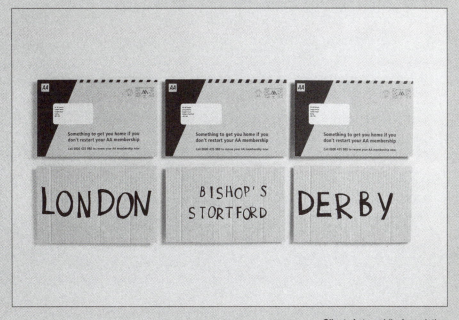

Client: Automobile Association
Agency: Harrison Troughton Wunderman
Art Director: Anthony Cliff
Copywriter: Stephen Timms
Creative Directors: Jack Nolan and Graham Mills
As shown in the *D&AD Annual 2002*

TARGETS

I've been asked many times, "which are the most important steps in creating a HEMP?" My answer, as you might expect, is "all of them" but steps four, five and six do stand out as being the most significant for many people.

Who are you targeting? Or put it another way, who is going to buy your product or service, or significantly influence the buyer? You need to know, and you need to be right. So often companies just don't know who they're selling to or don't know enough about them, and in my opinion you can't know too much.

If you're selling to the public are they rich or less well off? Young or old? Living in the north or south? Existing or new customers? And are they likely to be male or female? Do they know your product or service already? These are just the first group of questions, and if you don't know the answers then your marketing plan is going to be considerably less than highly effective.

What interests your targets? Which newspapers and magazines do they read? Where do they go on holiday? What income do they have? What do they like to spend their money on? Do they socialise a lot and, if so, do they eat out or entertain at home?

Of course everyone is different, and yet individuals share so many similarities. You have been on holiday and met like-minded people – is this a coincidence? You might be a member of a club, sporting, social or something else, and notice how many common interests you share with a number of the other members. Personally, one of my great loves is skiing and I've made many friends through this sport, some who at first glance are quite different and yet we have found so many common threads. They say that "birds of a feather flock together" – the same is also true of people. One of my former colleagues, Charles Smith, has a particular interest in identifying and classifying people and has come up with some amazing insights over the years. One day he told me how a recent survey revealed that people who buy brand new homes also tend to buy brand new cars, indeed on average their car is less than two years old. My first reaction was to say "that's about as relevant as 50% of married couples are female" until Charles pointed out that a nation-wide database exists of the people who own a car less than two years old. The direct mail campaigns which have followed this insight for a number of our house builder clients have proved to be very effective.

If you're selling to businesses, what type and size of business? Where are they based? And exactly whom in each organisation: the managing director, works manager or company buyer? What do these people currently have in common? What are their interests, both business and personal? Are they experiencing similar issues at work? Do they tend to be at the same stage of the business life cycle? Are they likely to be very IT literate for example, or Luddite in attitude? When you investigate your targets effectively you will discover so many similarities even if their businesses are in completely different sectors.

❝When you investigate your targets effectively you will discover so many similarities❞

TEC International, an organisation for Chief Executives from all sectors, is divided into groups of fifteen companies on a geographical basis. As these companies are all non-competing (they have to be due to the intimate nature of the TEC collective learning and developing process), you could imagine that there might not be a lot in common between the members. And yet, one of my great friends from TEC, Roger Gundry of IMG – Industrial Maintenance Group – and I have discovered over six years that our businesses are so alike in many ways. This is despite his manufacturing epoxy resins and my being in the business of communications! I've spoken to TEC groups up and down the UK and have observed how the common desire, to learn more effectively, has bonded together so many like-minded people.

Look beyond the obvious and continually ask questions – that is how you will discover the similarities. It's this information that will allow you to create a HEMP. Let's put it another way, are you going to be less effective if you know nothing about your targets – of course! So why do so many companies not bother to really get to know their customers? I remember doing business in the early 1980s and much of it was done over a long lunch or a game of golf. I think it was Michael Douglas in the film "Wall Street" who said "lunch is for wimps" and maybe this is partly why the current fashion is for meetings to be as short as possible and focused on a limited agenda. This practice is fine once you know each other, but it's very limiting don't you think? Spend some time with your clients with the sole purpose of getting to know them better, discover their ambitions, their outside work interests and what they're like as people. Take them out for lunch.

Another group of people to consider are those who have influence on your target. This could be work colleagues whose opinions your target values and who they consult with. It could be a supplier of other services whose recommendation is worth more than any promises you can make. What about at home? Don't underestimate the influence of husbands and wives, or children for that matter. I know very few people who don't discuss their work issues with their nearest and dearest from time to time, and their opinions count. You may find that until the more junior manager approves your proposal, the decision maker isn't even getting to hear of it. I cringe when hearing sales people say that they only deal with the decision maker, sometimes even asking a prospect if they have the authority to place an order. They might not have, but for sure they have the ability to make sure that your presentation is either rejected or qualified with a negative comment. Also have you noticed how often today's juniors become tomorrow's leaders? I know from bitter experience how easy it is to inadvertently upset the person who in a year's time will be renegotiating your contract!

You may find that you have several targets and they are quite different in many respects. If this is the case, you might need to create a separate HEMP from this point, for each of the targets. That's because the communication methods you will choose and indeed the message you will wish them to receive, might be quite different.

We created a HEMP for a brick manufacturer. This company specialises in handmade bricks which tend to look and feel much more attractive than those made by machines. However, they are considerably more expensive and, as their target companies' buyers were primarily interested in price, the company discovered how difficult it was to get onto the tender list, never mind win an order. Our HEMP resulted in a two-pronged attack. One set of communications was aimed at the marketing directors and Managing Directors of construction companies and showed how much better their properties would look with these more expensive bricks. The message was simple – spend a little more and be able to sell your now much more attractive properties for a considerable premium. At the same time, a campaign was directed at the buyers which talked about quality, consistency, ability to deliver on time, after-sales service and all the other issues buyers concern themselves with. Neither campaign on its own would have had the same effect and this insight came at this stage of the HEMP process, causing two plans to be created, albeit with a common desired result.

If you've got a number of different targets, select the most significant one for the rest of this HEMP, keeping the others in mind for the next steps, and then come back and continue the process, from this point, for each of the others. You may discover that your outcomes are similar or it may cause you to discard some targets in favour of others. Above all, I hope you won't compromise and end up talking to no-one as a consequence of trying to speak with everyone – a common mistake.

Example Redcup

Male finance directors aged between 40 and 55 of south-east based companies employing 50 or more employees on each site.

The Redcup directors knew who made the decision about coffee in companies – the finance director. That's because vending machines are normally leased and anything involving a legal contract usually ends up on the finance director's desk. Financial directors tend to be male and middle-aged and Redcup chose to focus on companies based in the south-east of England as initially its resources limited the geographical area it could cover to be within 50 miles of the Redcup office. Companies with less than 50 employees were less likely to be able to afford the investment of a Redcup machine so were not targeted specifically.

Incidentally, Redcup also identified facility managers as another target and subsequently developed a separate HEMP for this group. But for the purposes of this example we will focus on the finance directors only.

Often, you may find that you need to communicate with several target audiences for different reasons. In this instance, it may even be advisable to carry out separate HEMPs and then bring them together later. Redcup's primary target is obviously the people who watch the company purse strings, i.e. finance directors. As well as targeting these people directly, they can also be reached indirectly via the other company employees. If you target employees as a whole and interest them in your offer (thus instilling in them a desire for your product) then pressure to purchase will be exerted on your primary target (i.e. finance directors) through word-of-mouth, which is one of the most powerful marketing mediums. In this way, the employees have become a secondary target and one which is a much larger and less specific group than the primary target. Naturally, Redcup would need to use different marketing channels to communicate with these two audiences, in order to convey its message to both groups in the most effective and cost-effective way possible.

 # Word-of-mouth is one of the most powerful marketing mediums

HEMP STEP 4 Key points

- List out all your targets, being as specific as possible

- Describe what these people like and dislike, paint a really clear picture

- Your end targets might not be the people you need to get to – often it's key influencers who will communicate your message more effectively

HEMP in action — example 5

There are many advertisements and posters for jewellers. Typically they tend to show beautiful people wearing the latest jewellery design, and to be honest, it's difficult to tell one from another.

This creative treatment still highlights the product and yet does so with humour, something a lot of the most effective marketing campaigns utilise. This execution appeared on large posters, which can be a very cost-effective way of communicating an idea to a mass audience.

Client: Natan Jewellery
Agency: F/Nazca Saatchi & Saatchi
Creative Directors: Fabio Fernandes/Eduardo Lima
Art Director: Sidney Araújo
Copywriter: Eduardo Lima
Photographer: Fabio Bataglia
As shown in the *D&AD Annual 2003*

WHAT DO THEY CURRENTLY THINK AND DO?

What do your target(s) currently think and do in respect of your company, its products, its services and your desired result? It's very important to know how they think as it is this which causes them to act in the way they do. Thinking always precedes doing, so to make your targets do something different, something extra, you need to change the way they think first. And in order to change their thinking your starting point is, "What do they currently think?" And if you don't know, and I mean really know, then you need to find out.

Of course, if you ask someone "What do you think of me?" you might not always get an honest answer. People are, even today, still very polite and reluctant to upset you by being honest. Instead of saying something like "I don't think much of your service," they will say "I'm sure yours is very good but we're happy with our existing supplier." If you take this literally then you might implement a very different campaign to the one necessary to win the business. You know this to be true. And yet how many of us take what we're told as read, don't probe any further, and accept the feedback even if we know, deep down, that it's bull?

Recently, my team researched a company from top to bottom. We interviewed the Managing Director and, separately, the other directors. We met with senior, middle and junior managers as well as the teams on the front line. We conducted over 500 telephone interviews with previous and existing customers, and also carried out a similar survey of customers who use one of our client's competitors. The results were amazing, actually they were scary. The opinions of each group differed by miles. Customers used our client's services for totally different reasons to those they themselves believed. How on earth could it communicate effectively with such misalignment? The truth is that it didn't. Through another agency, not mine I hasten to add, they had spent in excess of £1million the previous year on an advertising campaign that not one, and I mean not one, of its customers had seen, or, if they had, they could not recall!

The point is that despite hundreds of daily interactions with customers nobody was doing anything about understanding their needs and desires. Everybody in this company had their own opinion and the more senior the person the more weight was given to their viewpoint. This happens, to one degree or another, in many companies and yet, speaking to customers, really finding out about them, is often cheap to do, easy to carry out and can reveal so many marketing opportunities. Why then don't companies understand their customers better? I don't know either, but hope that you will make the small effort required as part of your HEMP.

66Why don't companies understand their customers better?99

Of course, if you're starting up a new business then it's likely that no-one will know you or anything about you. This might appear to be a much better situation than the one established companies often face in trying to convert people who may already have negative views. It might appear that no research is required, but nothing could be further from the truth. You must learn, from day one, what customers want as your first impression, indeed early reputation, could be the make or break for you. So it is very important that you understand your targets. I suggest it's also very useful to understand what they don't like about your competitors. And please put to one side your own bias and truly listen to your targets, it's their opinion that matters.

If you don't know the answers to the above questions, if you don't know enough about your targets, and if you haven't got the time to find out yourself, then you need to invest money in research.

There are many different research companies who can help you but beware the bullshitters – there are loads out there. For example, we met a house builder who became a client after he spent £50,000 on research with a less than scrupulous "specialist". This research company's main conclusion was that people who moved home for discretionary reasons (i.e. those who were not moving for their career, expanding family, etc.) did so mainly because they wanted more space. Seriously, one research company charged £50,000 for this "insight"! You need to spell out exactly what you're expecting the research to accomplish and get the research company to write out exactly how it will go about the exercise. Also, get to see examples of its work and make sure that these are of the same type as the project you're embarking on.

A good advertising agency will be able to help you or you might want to think about how you can carry out research using your own resources. However, be careful if you go down this route, people often are reluctant to hear the truth about their own business and filter out all the stuff that needs to be acted on. If you take the in-house option, make sure that someone brave enough to tell it "as it is" heads up the team. This is not a job for the toadies!

Please consider this next point very carefully. You are not your target audience. Your opinion of your product or service is biased. Your colleagues, friends, family and suppliers are not your target audience either. They will not wish to hurt your feelings or may be indoctrinated by your passion, so that their opinion now is in alignment with your own. You need objective and accurate information about your target audience if you're going to communicate with them effectively. I believe that the primary reason companies go off track with their communications, and even with things like their product development, is because too many Chief Executives believe that they must be right and that their opinion is shared by everyone, or that people will eventually come round to see things their way. This is so dangerous and fuels so much waste – it borders on the criminal.

66Too many Chief Executives believe that they must be right99

Example Redcup

Typically, finance directors think that the kettle in the kitchen is perfectly adequate. So what they do is purchase instant coffee or tea bags as necessary. Those finance directors employing larger numbers of people tend to think that all vending machines are the same and therefore what they do is use the company that supplies the best deal (normally at the cheapest price).

The Redcup team knew their targets really well as they had dealt with them in their previous roles. Despite this, they chose to carry out research into the minds of finance directors (yes, I know), and gained some valuable ideas from the results. The big discovery was that finance directors hate being sold to in any way, (which they knew), but at the same time they wanted a lot of information in order to make an informed decision. The key was how to communicate without appearing to be selling, which we will look at later.

HEMP STEP **5** Key points

- Learn exactly what your targets currently think about you and your products and services
- If you don't know for certain then carry out research
- If you're brand new or unknown, then what do your targets think about your competitors?

HEMP in action   example 6

As with all these excellent examples of highly effective marketing in action, it's often the combination of the media chosen and the creative treatment which together makes the idea full of impact. This radio advertisement ran at busy rush hour times when it was likely that the target audience, car drivers, would be stuck in heavy traffic. The message that they might not be delayed if they were driving an Avensis is very compelling. Radio is often overlooked as a medium and yet it can be very powerful, talking to people when they're on their own and receptive to your message. The temptation, often, is to overload a radio advertisement with too much information. Instead, make it easy for listeners and make them want to find out more.

SFX: Office ambience (throughout).

MVO 1: What time's the client coming Dave?

MVO 2: Two o'clock.

MVO 1: That's OK we've got ages yet.

MVO 2: Yeah, have you heard how he speaks (*putting on ridiculous high-pitched voice*) "Hello Dave and how are you today?"

MVO 1: (giggling, also putting on ridiculous high-pitched voice) "I'm very well Peter and how are you?"

MVO 2: That's it (more giggling) "I'm very well and how are you today?"

MVO 1: "I'm very well Peter and how are you? No really how are you…"

SFX: Door opening.

MVO 2: "Shh, Shh."

MVO 1: (oblivious)… "And how are yooou? And how are you? And how are you? How are you? How…"

SFX: A long, uncomfortable pause.

Client: (in his own ridiculous high-pitched voice) "Hello David, how are you?"

MVO: The Toyota Avensis with electronic traffic avoidance system. Be careful. You might get there too early.

Client: Toyota (GB)
Agency: Saatchi & Saatchi
Directors: Hugh Todd and Adam Scholes
Copywriters: Hugh Todd and Adam Scholes
As shown in the *D&AD Annual 2002*

WHAT DO YOU WANT THEM TO THINK AND DO?

Stephen Covey offers the idea in his book *The Seven Habits of Highly Effective People* that everything is created twice – "mental creation precedes physical creation". If you want to change people, if you want them to do something different, if you want them to buy whatever it is you're selling, then first change the way they think. That's why, in the previous chapter, I urged you to discover what your target audience currently **thinks** as well as what they do. With this knowledge we can consider now what we want them to think instead. Once we change their thinking they will automatically change their doing.

> **❝**Once we change their thinking they will automatically change their doing**❞**

For some companies, start-ups for example, the targets will not be aware of your company and products and therefore what they currently do is buy from one of your competitors. On the face of it communicating with this group is a relatively easy job, just make the audience aware of your existence. If only it was this simple. Making them aware is one thing, but aware of what? Indeed, many well-established companies with products that are well-known, if not household names, can have an even more difficult task, that of changing their audience's views and mindset from one that is already deeply entrenched.

If your own opinion of your product or service is biased, and for 99% of us it is (yes, even you), then believe me when I say that your feelings towards your competitor's offering are even more clouded! And so, at the risk of appearing to be selling aggressively on behalf of research companies, please find out what your audience really thinks, not only about you but also about all of your competitors. Only then can you really begin to consider how you will go about changing their opinion, what they think, into what you want them to think. And then do.

I once worked with a client who believed his problem was that people thought his company too small to handle the really big projects. As a consequence, his team, who, as is so often the case, adopted his view as reality and only pursued small and medium-sized business projects. This, of course, fuelled the belief of everyone in the company even further – it would never win a big contract, you had to be a top five player to compete (my client wasn't even in the top ten of his industry based on size). It took a while to persuade this company to conduct research (after all it was totally convinced that after ten years there was nothing for it to learn). But when we interviewed thirty of its clients and a further thirty companies who hadn't used their services, a very different picture emerged. Over half believed that my client would be too expensive to handle the bigger projects, based on its higher per-centage charges for smaller jobs, and hence never considered the company. Size and scale of resources wasn't an issue for any of the people we met, indeed several companies told us that they would be delighted if my client would tender for the larger projects as the quality of its work was so high, but didn't believe that it wished to! How many limiting beliefs do you and your colleagues have which are holding you back I wonder?

Once you really know what your audiences are thinking you then need to consider what you want them to think instead. In many cases, it isn't a 180 degree shift. No, frequently it's more of a nudge on the tiller that's required, although in some extreme cases it can require a massive change of direction. There was a joke that did the rounds in the 1980s, (maybe even earlier), "What do you call a skip with wheels?" Answer, "a Skoda!" Recently, since being acquired by Volkswagen, Skoda has run a brilliant campaign, titled, "It's a Skoda, which for some people is still a problem." I don't know, but suspect, that it was debated at length whether the investment required to change people's perception of this East European car was worth it and instead should they just simply change the name? The fact is that here the company knew exactly what people thought of its cars, and as unpleasant as this must have been to accept, it bravely addressed the problem head-on and turned two decades of ridicule into a virtue. If the desired result is to sell more Skodas profitably, and that the start point was to change people's thinking from "the product's a joke" to "maybe it's worth considering at least" it's done a brilliant job. Indeed, Skoda achieved an all-time sales record in September 2003 with sales for that month increasing by 7.2% against a total market increase for the same month of only 1.6% (source: Skoda Press Office). Whilst this can be attributed, to a large extent, to the improvements in car design, build quality, specification and customer service, I suggest the real heroes are the people who changed the mind-set of Skoda customers. (And, in case you're wondering, I don't own a Skoda, nor can I imagine buying one, so Skoda's job isn't complete yet!)

 The real heroes are the people who changed the mind-set of Skoda customers

In this step of your HEMP you need to identify both what you want your targets to do and also, very importantly, how you want them to think. I repeat the point that the thinking will cause the doing. Now, let's consider for a moment what any communication, on its own, can achieve. How many people do you know believe that advertising, for example, sells the product or service? But you know better, don't you? In the majority of cases you're selling the idea of moving up the communication ladder, from see this ad, to make the call, to OK come and see me, to let's have a proposal, to yes I'll buy. Therefore what are you hoping your target will be thinking after seeing your communication? If your ambition is for your whole target audience to think "I love these people, I'll make them my suppliers for life and never have to see any of their competitors again," then, even with the most brilliant creative work, you're going to be disappointed. Instead, think about how your targets need to be thinking in order to get them to make the next step. It might be that they currently think, "I don't know about these people and what they're offering" and in this example it would be a real result to switch them to, "I'm interested in these people, I like what they're saying, and I'll certainly see them at least."

As you will see from the Redcup example, this HEMP step is where the biggest insight comes into play, indeed these two chapters are probably the most important when it comes to getting really effective with your marketing campaign. I've shown below, both the initial thinking of the Redcup team, and the subsequent post-research idea.

Example Redcup (one)

"Excellent beverages contribute positively to the overall office environment. The kettle isn't adequate, we need a better, albeit more expensive, solution. I've heard that Redcup are the number one suppliers of quality coffee for the workplace. I'll get them in for a chat."

Example Redcup (two)

"My people are spending up to an hour a day visiting Starbucks and other cafés. This is costing us a fortune! I need to find an alternative method of providing coffee in our offices. I've heard that Redcup are the number one suppliers of quality coffee for the workplace, I'll get them in for a chat."

The Redcup team, despite thinking they knew their targets, discovered that they didn't really understand them. Most finance directors aren't interested in the office environment and certainly aren't likely to fork out cash on extravagances such as coffee machines. But they are interested in money – both making it and, of even more interest for the majority, in saving it. And once the Redcup team understood this their whole approach changed. No longer were they going to "up sell", which is one of the hardest sells anyway. Instead they had got an idea that they knew really appealed to their targets (better coffee will actually save money), an idea they could communicate in highly effective ways. And they did!

HEMP STEP 6 Key points

- Thinking always precedes doing so understand what you want your targets to think
- And then what you want them to do

HEMP in action   example 7

Car theft is a big problem in South Africa. As with most problems, this creates an opportunity – one for which Hollard Insurance has provided a solution. Its advertisement in *Autotrader* features photographs of empty garages and driveways taken in the same style as the "amateur" shots of the cars for sale which appear throughout the magazine. The advertisement is totally focused on the issue its target audience needs to consider very carefully, at exactly the right time, and in a way that must cause the reader to say "how clever".

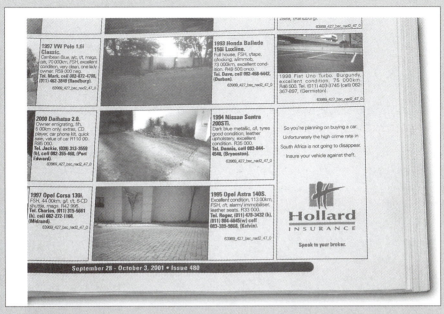

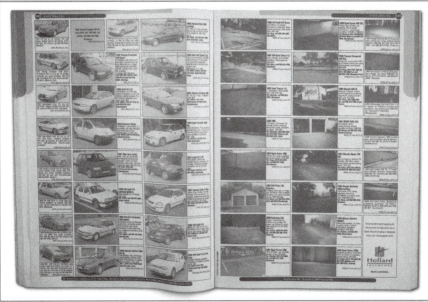

Client: Hollard Insurance
Art Director: Tom Cullinan
Copywriters: Tom Cullinan and Mike Ellman-Brown
Creative Director: Mike Schalit
Photographer: Tom Cullinan
As shown in the *D&AD Annual 2002*

WHAT'S THE STORY?

Iknow that you, like me, have experienced that really uncomfortable feeling when someone is still talking, without pausing, and you're none the wiser, in response to your question, "So what is it you do?"

We've all experienced this situation and have fought that glazing-over feeling indicating just how uninteresting we're finding this person and their business. And yet, they probably do have something to offer, as of course you do too. Why is it then that so many people can't express themselves clearly, particularly given that we're all asked this question regularly, if not several times a day?

You may have heard the elevator speech story before but it's worth retelling it to reinforce this point. Many years ago, in Wall Street, there were just a handful of people who had the power and influence to make or break a new venture, approve or reject a finance proposal, cause a company share price to soar or plummet. These market makers were very difficult to get to – they had an army of receptionists, secretaries and assistants whose first priority was to "shield the boss". An appointment with one of these financial gods was as rare as a teenager without a mobile phone. However, their fortress-like protection had a chink; an Achilles heel which once a day left them exposed ... but only for one and a half minutes. Like so many others who are important, one of these men had offices on the top floor of a skyscraper and every day took a lift ride of roughly ninety seconds duration. Anybody else could share that particular lift and so had this short period of time to make their pitch: less than two minutes to gain his attention, capture his interest and stimulate his desire to learn more. Imagine yourself in that position. How would you start your "presentation"? What would you particularly emphasise? Which of your product or service features and benefits would you amplify? And which would you leave out? How would you bring the pitch to a close? What would you say to leave your audience gagging for more?

"What would you say to leave your audience gagging for more?"

Think about it: if you can't describe, compellingly, your business to an audience of one, how on earth can you expect a group of people, possibly thousands, to understand or be interested in your advertisement or other communication?

I know this is obvious, indeed blindingly so. I know that it's so straightforward everyone "gets it" immediately. So try this out. Open any newspaper or magazine and you will find several advertisements with completely unintelligible messages, filled with assumptions of understanding, industry jargon and totally lacking in motivation for you to *do* something. It's quite incredible how inept so many companies are at describing what they do in a language that their target audience will understand and be excited about.

How many presentations have you received in the last six months where you clearly understood everything? How many told you exactly the information you wanted to know about? How many caused you to buy? I meet hundreds of people who bore me witless, (the editor wouldn't allow me my rhyming couplet here), and yet, when I can be bothered to explore more, not least when I'm engaged to help them with their communications, I discover how remarkable they and their companies are. But so many people just don't know how to tell their story or, worse, can't abridge it to ninety seconds.

So, before we start to consider how to communicate to our target audience, the next stage of your HEMP is to write out exactly what you do. You might like to take a piece of paper and start writing. Imagine that the person you'll send this to has no idea whatsoever of your business sector, your products and services, what the features and benefits are – in fact, imagine they've been in a twenty-year coma and know nothing of the developments in your industry over the last two decades.

Make sure you include background information about your company. Write an exact description of what each of your products and services actually do. Include an analysis of how these differ from, and are better than, your competitors', and also which features and benefits your competitors have that you don't. And be honest – remember this is your plan and unless you choose to show it, no-one else will see it!

The next stage, having captured all the detail, is to start editing. The first things to delete are statements such as "highest quality", "best service", which cannot be genuinely substantiated. Next, take out all the corporate babble – your audience doesn't want to hear it. Next, remove all jargon and detailed descriptions of machinery or processes – again they're not interested. Confine your script to the "meat and potato" – you can add the trimmings when your, interested, audience asks for them.

"Take out all the corporate babble – your audience doesn't want to hear it"

Example Redcup

Redcup is a new company, although the directors have many years' experience of providing drink vending machines to offices and other workplace environments. Redcup is different because it supplies café-quality coffee and other beverages to offices. Redcup machines ensure that fresh coffee beans are individually ground for each and every cup. Espresso, Latte Macchiato, Cappuccino and Americano are all available from Redcup machines at the touch of just one button and can be decaffeinated or freshly made with skimmed milk if preferred. It takes less than ten seconds (on average) to create a delicious Redcup coffee. Redcup provides a total service including the installation and daily maintenance of the machines, sourcing and supplying all consumables for a pre-agreed fixed price. All Redcup products are sourced with the environment in mind and most coffee beans are "fair trade". All components used by Redcup are recyclable and the company makes sure that all packaging etc. is properly managed.

With Redcup, your company will have more motivated employees, who will never again experience the 'plastic' after-taste of vended drinks. Clients will love visiting your offices; in fact you may find that many will just "drop in for a coffee". Redcup is revolutionising the office beverage market and is setting a new and much higher standard for workplace refreshments.

HEMP STEP 7 Key points

- State in as few words as possible what it is your products and services actually do
- Cut out all the peripheral stuff
- Keep focused on the "meat and potato" of your offer

HEMP in action example 8 overleaf

I'm very happy to promote a competitor when they do something that I wished I'd thought of. Claire Inc. stationery is in the form of a radio script and guess what it does? Another class piece of communication which costs nothing (it needed stationery anyway).

Business Card 30"

FVO:	*(Warm but confident delivery.*
	Background music under throughout.)
	Hi there. It's me Claire from **Claire inc.** The producer in Radio & Music Producer. The specialist in African Production
	Specialist. And the flippin' as in flippin' hot person for the job.
SFX:	*(Sound of telephone ringing.)*
FVO:	Give me a buzz on 083 260 2131 or clairebell1@hotmail.com
ANNCR:	Claire inc. Anything but background noise.

Compliment Slip 30"

FVO:	*(Warm but confident delivery. Background music under throughout.)*
	Hi there. It's me again. Claire from **Claire inc.** Thank you for using my services. You've been a super cool client. Until next time. Cheers for now.
SFX:	*(Sound of clinking glasses.)*
FVO:	Keep it handy – 083 260 2131 or clairebell1@hotmail.com
ANNCR:	Claire inc. Anything but background noise.

Letterhead 30"

FVO: *(Warm but confident delivery. Background music under throughout.)*
Hi there. It's me Claire from **Claire inc.** The producer in Radio & Music Producer.
The Specialist in African Production Specialist. And the flippin' as in flippin' hot person for the job.
SFX: *(Sound of telephone ringing.)*
FVO: Give me a buzz on 083 260 2131 or clairebell1@hotmail.com
ANNCR: Claire inc. Anything but background noise.

Client: Claire Inc.
Design Groups: Saatchi & Saatchi (Cape Town) & Eye Design Studio
Design Director: Isaac February
Designer: Gavin Bloys
Copywriter: Razzia Essack
As shown in the *D&AD Annual 2002*

YOUR ONE BIG THING (AKA THE TEN-SECOND SELL)

Step seven caused you to stop and think about your business and to write out everything you do. Whilst this is probably very factual and complete it might not necessarily be compelling for your audience, indeed it probably tells not sells. The Redcup example still contains too much information for an elevator speech, and certainly is far too long for an advertisement. So what you now need to do is to identify what it is, above all else, that makes your product and service so special. What's your one big thing?

Sometimes companies lose sight of why their customers buy from them, as a consequence of being so wrapped up in themselves. This seems particularly true when a product or service is continuously developed and improved until the original function appears forgotten. Also, companies can get blinded by competitors and believe that they have to out-improve them, when actually often all the customer really wants is the original product at a cheaper price.

So why should someone buy from you? What is the one reason, above all others, that should make them buy?

Pearson, my publisher, tests authors by asking them to write out, in no more than ten seconds, why their book will sell. This can be quite challenging, to say the least, but it's a very good exercise at cutting to the chase.

So having written a ninety-second pitch the next step is to write a ten-second one. The key objective here is to state something that will cause your target audience to ask you a follow-up question, such as "How?" or "Go on" giving you permission to feed them, piece by piece, your incredible story. (It is an incredible story, isn't it?)

> ❝Having written a ninety-second pitch the next step is to write a ten-second one❞

Try this idea if you're struggling a little. Have you ever done telesales? If not, can you picture just how difficult this method of communication is, particularly if you're not really well prepared? However, if you know that what you have to say works, because you've done it successfully fifty times that week, how much better will your next call be? Let's pretend that you're about to pick up the phone and cold call your number one target and pitch your proposition. What will you say? How will you make sure that you don't hear the words "not interested", "leave me alone", or "(pick your expletive) off"! Now, as you consider this, you may already have had an idea about what you can say that will get you past the crucial ten-second point.

Example Redcup

Redcup will put Starbucks in your office.

(And that's a three-second sell!)

Your one big thing doesn't need to tell the whole story; indeed this is where people so often go wrong. Instead it's much better to get them on the hook by dangling the bait of the one big thing, causing them to utter the magical phrase, "That's interesting, tell me more." I know of no better sentence in the salesman's handbook, other than perhaps, "Please can I have some," or "Where do I sign?"

> ❝The magical phrase,
> 'That's interesting, tell me more.'❞

The Redcup example illustrates very well how less is more. The borrowed image of an actual Starbucks replacing a drab kitchen or drinks point within an office is very powerful. All the other great things Redcup do, such as sourcing their coffee from fair trade growers, etc. adds excellent detail once the prospect is on the hook.

HEMP STEP 8 Key points

- Summarise in ten seconds or less what you do in a compelling way
- Rather than tell the whole story create a statement that leaves your audience wanting more
- Make sure that this message comes across in all communications

HEMP in action example 9

It's hard to stand out on New Bond Street in London. Some of the world's most beautiful and luxurious products are retailed there and, as they sit side by side, it's difficult to achieve prominence. Mulberry managed it though. With brilliant timing, this hoarding went up during London Fashion Week, clearly communicating the future store opening. I'm amazed how often companies ignore opportunities to promote themselves via their own buildings etc – here's an example to motivate you.

Client: Mulberry
Design Group: Four IV Design Consultants
Designers: Kim Hartley and Paul Skerm
As shown in the *D&AD Annual 2002*

WHAT'S THE BENEFIT OF THAT?

Have another look at your one big thing. Does it turn your prospect on, or is it something innocuous like "leading service" or "high quality" which everyone can and does claim? Also, is your one big thing benefiting you or your customer more? For example, some companies get really excited about their processes or high-tech equipment, whereas the customer really couldn't care less so long as the product arrives on time in the condition they expect. For all I know, Amazon might just have the most advanced computerised warehouse in the world – not interested! But I love it when they deliver my book the next day, at a cheaper price and gift wrapped too if I'm in the mood! Your one big thing is actually your customers one big thing – they own it after you've created it. As you know, customers create brands, companies just provide the framework, impetus and continuous development – if they're really clever. Unfortunately too many businesses believe that they can dictate to their customers how they should feel about their products and services, and ninety-nine times out of a hundred, no matter how much they spend, this is just not possible.

Ideally your one big thing should be motivating to customers on both a rational and emotional level, something that makes them smile when they first hear it.

"Your one big thing should be motivating to customers on both a rational and emotional level"

Of course, if your one big thing isn't pressing your customers' buttons you know what to do, don't you? That's it, come up with something else, otherwise all that money of yours that you're going to spend on communications will be wasted. This book is all about highly-effective marketing, not fast ways to blow some cash on advertising a poor, tired product. There's an old saying, so old I don't know who said it first, that "great advertising helps a bad product to fail faster". You must make sure that whatever you're communicating is appealing to the audience you're after. Rarely is this your CEO, wife, boyfriend or mother. Almost never is it you.

Of course, today's new features are tomorrow's standard items. Imagine in 1979 having to buy a heated rear windscreen device from Halfords for you to install yourself on your brand new Mini! Not to mention buying a radio and having to drill a hole in the bodywork to fit the aerial yourself as well! You need to make sure that your "one big thing" of last year is still compelling. And this demonstrates again why continuous dialogue with customers is so valuable. Your target audience knows better than you whether they're turned on by what you have to offer. All too often companies rely on the big thing of yesteryear and in today's world, this just isn't good enough. Let's face facts, almost everything can be, and is, copied within months, weeks, even days. I heard Charles Dunstone of the Carphone Warehouse speak at his business conference, monitoring the prices of all their competitors, across Europe, every hour of every day!

As I've said, your one big thing will have an emotional benefit which will resonate with your targets. The best ones get to clients deep inside. There are many great examples of this. Take Apple. Many of its customers really love its products – "I love my Mac" is something I've heard many times, and although I don't use one myself (currently using a really cool laptop/tablet combined by Toshiba if you're interested), my iPod, with over 200 albums downloaded on it, and still bags of room for more, is just the trippiest thing in my life at the moment (sad I know). It just blows me away. I can talk about it for hours but haven't felt compelled to have its logo tattooed on my body, yet! Which of course no-one in their right mind would do – would you? And so you can't be the owner of a Harley Davidson motorcycle because this is what some of their adoring customers do. Not a handful either, hundreds of them; so many there's an annual competition for the most creative body art!

I love my "Camelbak" rucksack with its three-litre reservoir that enables me to cycle for three hours or more without stopping or swerving dangerously when I need a drink. I love it. I love my "Bose Wave" CD/Radio – how can something so small sound so orchestral? I love my Aeron chair by Herman Miller and I love Saag Gosht from the Bombay Bicycle Club – the best Indian restaurant in London (in my biased opinion). I love my favourite photograph of my daughter in its beautiful David Linley frame, and I love my original 1920s anglepoise lamp by Herbert Terry. You get my drift don't you? And it's not just products that get me excited to an almost dangerous level – I get as carried away by great service too. I love Ariel Miller the best ski teacher in Vail (and owner of a "five counties butt" – which I'll happily follow down any run, however extreme). I love Andy of Autovalet who's cleaned my car every Monday, without fail, for seven years. I love Douglas & Gordon estate agents (yes, it is possible to love an estate agent), because they're the nicest people you could ever deal with and when you're buying or selling your most valuable asset you want to deal with someone you can trust, someone you like. I love Neil Taylor of Spectron, whose team have installed electrics and telephone systems in hundreds of buildings for me, both offices and homes, with a service level that goes beyond legendary. There are hundreds of products and services you love – so how many customers love yours?

Another sales pitch for more research! When did you last ask your customers why they buy from you? Exactly. Research doesn't have to be expensive but is frequently very valuable. Consider the example of Lisa Baldwin. Prior to taking her brilliant dance school for kids, Poptastic, nationwide, she asked all the parents of her first group why they paid for their children to come to her classes. The insights included several things which Lisa had suspected but not realised the value of, such as allowing shy and less confident children the opportunity to socially interact without the pressures of school or the competitive nature of sport. Now think about this. Lisa's classes were over subscribed by 200% with a twelve-month waiting list. Many people would, indeed some did, suggest that research wasn't necessary. However, given her ambition for Poptastic to be an international brand, she wanted to find out exactly what made her classes so popular. As an aside she also managed to get a near 100% return of questionnaires by asking questions of both the children and their parents and getting the kids to nag the parents for answers. And she obtained over a hundred quotes from kids and their parents to be used for future marketing purposes.

" When did you last ask your customers why they buy from you? "

Example Redcup

Redcup saves companies a fortune by stopping employees wasting valuable time visiting cafés. Redcup coffee makes you more money because it's so good customers will find reasons to make extra visits.

These are the two key customer benefits Redcup highlights – saving money and making money. I know of few more powerful. Of course, your customer benefit doesn't have to be financial but, as with your desired result (see steps one and two), if you can drill down to a monetary value this is going to help you significantly.

HEMP STEP 9 Key points

- Things which benefit you might not always benefit your customer
- Check that your "ten-second sell" (step eight), has real benefit for your customer

HEMP in action   example 10

By now you'll have got the message that it's not just the creative idea which makes for Highly Effective Marketing – it's also about the choice of media and the timing. What do you sit on when watching TV? Right, so consider just how clever the ad for Reebok UK is. Titled "escape the sofa" I wonder how many people decided there and then not to put that run off until tomorrow?

Client: Reebok UK
Agency: Lowe
Director: Frank Budgen
Modelmaker: Asylum Models & Effects
Copywriter: Tony Barry
Art Director: Vince Squibb
Creative Director: Paul Weinberger
As shown in the *D&AD Annual 2002*

KNOW YOURSELF

So far you've addressed a lot of 'whats'? What you want, what product and service you offer, what the one big thing you have is, what benefits this has for your customers? Now you need to take a good look at yourself in a different way – Who are you?

In the same way everybody has a personality, so do all companies. Some are traditional, solid and safe as houses. Others are cool, trendy even funky. A number are highly professional and quite technical, whilst quite a few are easily excitable, loud and boisterous (think packed out Italian restaurant on a Friday night). No personality is necessarily always right or wrong. I'm not advocating that all companies should be cutting-edge cool. Indeed I can think of little worse than a trendy and slightly funky undertaker!

The most important thing is that your company personality is one which appeals to your main target audience. And it must be consistent. After all, very rarely do you like people with a split personality, and just as bad are those who try to be one thing to some people and something else to another – it's so obvious and unattractive.

Often I find that companies know that their personality isn't quite right and search for ways of changing easily. There aren't many ways, it's difficult. However, the results more than reward the effort as French

Connection United Kingdom discovered after re-branding themselves as FCUK. But it's not just about a change of name or logo, or even new or different products and services, although these things can help enormously. No, this step is about making sure that your business is projecting the right personality which, when you think about it, is so important.

❝'People buy people first' is another old cliché. And truism❞

"People buy people first" is another old cliché. And truism. You forgive people you like more easily. You look forward to meeting friends in business and hope they've got something good for you. Consider the opposite point of view. Someone you really don't like at all is underperforming – how do you treat them? A supplier of an excellent product is coming to see you, but he's plain ignorant and rude – are you looking forward to hearing his pitch? You may buy what he's selling because you need it today, but there will come a time when someone else can service your need – and how much do you look forward to that day? And this isn't just about the extremes, like and dislike, good or bad, it's not black and white. In the shades of grey are many types of feelings ranging across the scale and what tips the balance one way or the other, so frequently in buying decisions, is the personality of the company.

If you don't really know what the personality for your company is, or indeed what you'd like it to be, one useful exercise is to compare your business with others from different sectors. For example if your company was an airline, would you be more like:

- British Airways
- Virgin Atlantic
- Singapore Airlines
- Easy Jet
- Ryanair
- A private Gulfstream G5?

If you compare yourselves to a TV company would it be:

- BBC
- CBBC
- ITV
- Sky
- Channel 4
- Bravo
- Channel 5
- MTV?

Or how about a food retailer:

- Tesco
- Sainsbury's
- Marks & Spencer
- BP filling station
- Fortnum & Mason
- Planet Organic
- Waitrose
- Your local convenience store on the corner?

Cars and other methods of transport are often used as a way of illustrating how different personalities can be adopted:

- Mercedes Benz
- Hyundai
- Rolls-Royce
- Porsche
- Audi
- Ferrari
- Ford
- the 319 double-decker bus
- The Paris Metro (surely you wouldn't compare yourself to the tube)?

How about clothing?

- Saville Row
- Next
- Armani
- Gap
- FCUK
- charity shop
- Diesel?

All of these examples illustrate how no one way is right or another is wrong when it comes to personality. Of course, I should have said this earlier, please choose your own list of comparisons and add any company you like to the lists above: it's your choice of personality for your company that matters. When you've considered your comparison companies then ask yourself, why? What is it that makes my business like the xyz company? What are the visible similarities? And what are the less tangibles, the feelings that dealing with xyz gives me, which in turn I hope to give others? And then write those words down. Capture the feelings. Express why xyz is just so damn great. Because it's this you will want to share, not the names of the comparison companies as these will mean different things to different people. I love Oddbins but a colleague of mine doesn't, despite the fact that we both love companies that are slightly quirky, unconventional, which supply products we weren't expecting.

What matters is that you know your personality and then, when you do really know who you are, you can apply it to everything.

Have you flown with British Airways and Virgin Atlantic? Both give safety briefings prior to departure (all airlines have to under CAA law), and both have the same content including the amusing "ladies remove high heeled shoes" as if this will be something you consider in the last few seconds before impact! However, both BA and Virgin deliver the message in a different way, absolutely reflecting their personality. BA always has the captain or first officer start proceedings by asking you to pay attention to Keith or Sharon the cabin director, in a very clipped tone, typical of that company's way of doing things. Virgin on the other hand (and I'm very happy for you to notice my preference and total admiration for Sir Richard), have a video cartoon with a superb range of voiceovers including Leslie Phillips as the captain "Hellooo, and aren't you looking good today" followed by John Hannah, the actor who played the younger gay guy in "Four Weddings and a Funeral", as the steward – masterful casting. Virgin knows who it is and what its personality is all about. For example, a while back I was fortunate to travel Upper Class to LA and, before take off, was offered a choice of either champagne or fresh orange juice. I asked, "Would it be a complete pain to have a bucks fizz?", "Yes," said the cabin crew member "it would, but now you've asked I'm going to get you one" (with a huge smile). Everything Virgin does is in alignment with its personality. Its style of letter writing, for example, is open, friendly; I'd describe it as casual as opposed to formal. Whereas BA is the opposite, it's so straight it makes me feel like I'm dealing with an old-fashioned lawyer. To be fair to BA, it is consistently pompous and arrogant and is so good at it that I have to conclude it has this as a deliberate choice of personality: it cannot be possible to achieve this level of consistency otherwise!

But can you see how companies can provoke such reactions from people? I positively choose to fly with another airline rather than BA, not because of its safety record or lack of destinations – they fly to more places than most – or because BA's more expensive or some other tangible. No, I dislike BA's personality and it's this that costs it several thousand pounds a year which I spend with other airlines.

I suspect I'm not BA's target audience (and am even less likely to be after this diatribe), and if that's the case then well done BA!

Think about the companies you like (and dislike too). You'll notice how the good ones do things in a manner that is predictable and in alignment. Your business can have these traits too – all you have to do is define them and then live them.

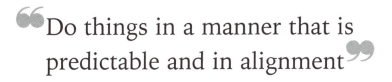

Do things in a manner that is predictable and in alignment

I suggest you start by identifying the personality you desire for your business and then carry out an honest critique of how it is at this moment in time. If there's no gap, or if you have a start-up company, then lucky you! However, if, as is the case for many of us, there is a crack, cavern or gulf between the current and the desired personality, you've got your work cut out. But at least you'll know what you're working towards.

I believe that whilst we all create something different there are many pioneers we can learn from, companies that have already been through this process. You'll find many of these companies will be extremely helpful. If you write to them explaining what a fan you are and how you would like to learn more about them you'll be very pleasantly surprised how many will invite you to visit and learn more. And that's when you can find out how they actually go about creating their personalities, which is, after all, as a consequence of the way in which they do things.

❝There are many pioneers we can learn from❞

A starting point for your search is the usual obvious place – the web. Also, consider getting hold of a company's annual Report and Accounts if it's a quoted company. Another way to find out more is to contact their PR agency and ask for information; again you'll find most will be helpful.

Once you've worked out who to emulate, and why, identify up to ten words that describe your desired personality. This is helpful because different people don't all share the same views about companies and see different things. What matters is how you want your business to be seen by your target audiences, which of course include the people who you work with as well. In fact, this group is just as important, as it will deliver your personality.

Example Redcup

Redcup is Virgin Atlantic, Diesel, Mini Cooper S, Planet Organic. That's because Redcup is young, bold, fun, iconoclastic and revolutionary.

Redcup, being a start-up business, could choose whoever it liked to emulate and, of course, its own personal, individual personalities come into the equation. But it went a step further and also looked at its competitors, not just in respect of their product and service offerings, but also at each competitor's personality. Redcup discovered that no vending company had any of the characteristics which it has now chosen and created. This helped the selection considerably as, by being a bit radical, and some might say off the wall, Redcup makes a first impression which will be remembered. You might like to take a good look at your competitors as well. If they are all acting in the same or in a very similar way with the same character traits this presents you with a fantastic opportunity.

HEMP STEP 10 Key points

- Every company has a personality – what's yours?
- Your personality needs to appeal to your target audience – if it doesn't then change your personality – it's easier than changing your customers
- Make sure that your personality is consistent and comes across in all communications

HEMP in action   example 11

David Howlett and Matthew Peckham, students at Central St Martins College of Art and Design, created this brilliant idea for TV Licensing to consider. If you received this and you hadn't bought a TV licence it would make you think, wouldn't it? And more importantly, having made you think differently from "they'll never catch me" to "crikey they're on to me" this would make you do something different – like buy a TV licence.

91 Eswyn Road
London, SW17 8TR

maxell

AHA, SO YOU'VE DEFINITELY
GOT A TELLY THEN.

THE QUESTION IS, HAVE
YOU GOT A LICENCE FOR IT?

IF THE ANSWER'S NO, MAYBE
IT'S TIME YOU THOUGHT
ABOUT GETTING ONE

BECAUSE IT'LL COST YOU
A GRAND IF YOU HAVEN'T

AND WE KNOW WHERE
YOU LIVE.

T✓
LICENSING

Pay by post, telephone, direct debit or online.
0800 123 4567

Students: David Howlett and Matthew Peckham
Tutors: Clive Challis, Maggie Gallagher and Zelda Malan
College: Central St Martins College of Art and Design
As shown in the *D&AD Annual 2002*

HOW WILL YOU TALK TO YOUR TARGETS?

Many companies bypass the first ten steps of HEMP and come straight **here.** They think they know everything so far and the only issue therefore is how they're going to communicate with their target audience. That's why so many of today's communications are crap, wasteful and actually harmful. But you know better, so having completed your HEMP this far, it's time to consider how you will get your message to your target audience in the most effective way(s) possible.

In order to do this we're going to have a look at some of the different methods of communication and consider the pros and cons for each. Some of you will know this stuff so please feel free to skip to the next step, although for many others, I'm told this will be very useful.

TV advertising

Advertising used to be, and for some still is, a catch-all term for communications. But our definition is "paid for" media. This includes TV (terrestrial, satellite and digital); radio; press, including trade, classified, run of paper, regional, local and national; posters of all shapes and sizes; and cinema.

Advertising agencies like advertising – a lot. So do many clients. It's very visible and expensive and can be highly creative. "Advertising has made many companies what they are today" is a popular mantra for many who still believe its magical powers are intact. Trust me, they're not. If you're over 30 you'll remember the TV ads of your childhood because they were so memorable. Not necessarily because they were brilliantly creative, although a number were, but because you saw them so often. With only a choice of three or four TV stations, or sides as we used to call them ("what side is it on?"), and only two of these having ads, at least 50% of your total audience could be guaranteed near as damn it to see your ad if you ran it often enough. The same is not true today. Video didn't kill the radio star but it seriously wounded ads. Likewise satellite and digital exploded the choices available to over 100+ channels (most of which are garbage but that's another subject), and therefore you could no longer rely on half the country seeing your ad during "News at Ten". In fact, today, on average only 18% of the viewing public (3.5 million viewers – source: BARB 2003) watch this programme regularly compared with 34% ten years ago (6.6 million viewers – source: BARB 1993). TV advertising can also be expensive, although one of the benefits of specialised channels is the ability to more accurately target your audience(s) – assuming of course that you know who they are (see HEMP step four), and that they are a specific group. If your targets are everyone aged between five and seventy-five, of all socio-economic categories, across every geographical area (think Coca-Cola) then you have a problem. Which is why Coca-Cola and others still invest millions of pounds every year in TV advertising.

❝Advertising agencies like advertising – a lot❞

The old rules no longer apply. TV advertising does not have the same effect it used to and yet there are upsides for you to consider. Previously it was prohibitively expensive, and only a tiny percentage of companies could afford it. Today it's available to many more of us, so long as we are very targeted, at a fraction of the price. You might not have considered TV advertising before – maybe it's time to start.

Cinema

Do you love the cinema? Imagine your advertisement appearing on the big screen with full-on Dolby Digital Surround Sound! Looks and sounds great doesn't it? Although cinema as a medium is not going to deliver you the kind of mass audiences that terrestrial TV channels can conjure up, you may find that a cinema audience is in a more receptive frame of mind for viewing your ad, therefore making it more effective. To start with, cinemagoers are voluntarily trapped in a seat in a darkened theatre so your ad is all they have to focus on as opposed to the million and one other things people may be doing at home whilst they've got one eye on the TV. Moreover, in a recent survey, 47% of the people questioned agreed that "cinema adverts and trailers were part of the entertainment" (source: CAA/CAVIAR 20 (2002)). The good news for this sector is that cinema viewing is on the increase – 2002 saw the highest admissions since the 1970s (176 million – source: CAA/CAVIAR 20 (2002) / Nielsen EDI) and 26% of the population now visit the cinema on a regular monthly basis. Compare this with ten years ago when only 11% of the population were regulars (source: CAA/CAVIAR 20 (2002)).

Cinema advertising can be quite targeted because you can select the films which your ad will precede, so, for instance, if you're selling a new toy, advertising prior to the latest Disney release is going to give you a targeted audience. Unsurprisingly, advertising before the biggest blockbusters is always more expensive than those quaint, arty, French, budget productions which get the great reviews but few bother with. Cinema advertising is also capable of being purchased regionally (hence all those Chinese restaurant ads). At the end of the day, it's important to consider the mood of your audience and ask yourself whether they are going to be more interested in your product if they've gone to watch a sci-fi flick or a slapstick comedy. Bear in mind that creative directors of ad agencies tend to love cinema more than any other medium, because their work is being inflated to silver screen status, side by side with Tarantino, Scorsese or Spielberg – and if that isn't an ego trip . . . . Having said that, it can be a cost effective way of making a big splash with your message to a small but highly targeted and predisposed audience.

Radio

Radio is still overlooked by many and it shouldn't be. It has an obvious disadvantage, as students of neuro-linguistic programming or NLP will know, given that many people have a preference to receive information visually. Many advertisers believe that so much of their brand value and image is invested in the visual (i.e. logo, packaging, product shot), that they can't afford to sacrifice this element and trust to sound waves alone. However, because the brand image becomes invisible on radio, the advertiser can concentrate instead on projecting its brand character, thus forming a more emotional and personal relationship with its target audience. Some advertisers make the most of this unique medium and treat listeners to brilliant creative work which conjures up vivid mental pictures from sounds, but so often this potential is wasted and radio ads sound as inane as disc jockey babble that listeners filter out between tracks of music.

66 Forming a more emotional and personal relationship 99

With over 200 local stations, commercial radio is still largely region-alised (although there are around fifteen national stations including

Classic FM and Virgin FM) and consequently can be used cost effectively to communicate to a broad audience within a defined geographical region. Commercial radio started in 1973 with only three stations. Today there are nearly 230 (source: RAJAR) achieving a 96% coverage of the population (source: RAJAR 1994). Many of these differentiate themselves through their broadcast output, largely music or news, and as a result, attract different audience profiles. So, radio offers you the ability to speak to your target(s) by age and by region at a fraction of the price of TV advertising. And, as many people listen to the radio in their cars at "drive time", your audience is a captive one.

The future looks bright for radio – there has been a huge increase over the past twenty-five years in the amount of time adults spend listening to the radio (140% increase from 1975 to 1994 – source: JICRAR/RAJAR). What is more, according to research carried out in 2002 by media buying agency, Carat, television viewing has declined significantly while radio listening is on the increase.

As with TV, radio can be used both as a brand-building medium and tactically to promote a special promotion. The most effective advertisers tend to use radio a lot, recognising that they can build a relationship with their targets over time.

Example **Redcup**

Overleaf is the script for a Redcup radio commercial.

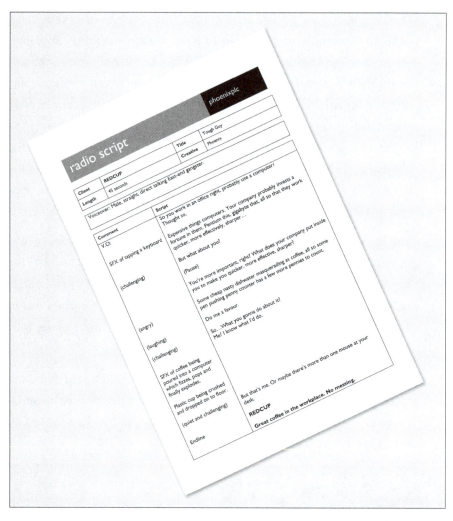

Client: Redcup
Agency: Phoenix

Posters

Posters are great. Massive images, lots of colour, highly visible and huge impact. But again, there are downsides. As most people view them at 30+mph they can't contain a lot of information, or if they do, trust me, it's not recalled. Until recently posters were the only advertising medium which tobacco companies had access to and they consequently pushed the price of sites sky high. There has been little reduction since, however, largely because other mediums, particularly TV, are less effective than they used to be, so volume advertisers have filled the vacuum. On the face of it, posters could be used for a very targeted campaign in one or more regions, but the major companies who own the majority of all poster sites prefer to sell packages of sites to volume advertisers and whilst you can cherry pick, (every site has its own unique reference number), it's very expensive to do so.

As a rule, if you're using posters keep it simple. Less is more. Rarely do creative executions for one medium, press advertising for example, translate without amendment to posters. Instead please view them separately and allow any temptation to tell the whole story to be resisted.

"If you're using posters keep it simple. Less is more"

Press advertising

Press advertising is possibly the most hit and miss communications media. Advertisers are often blind to the differences between run of paper and classified press media. Consider this point: unless you've changed jobs recently, when did you last read the job advertisements? So when you're not looking for a new job you don't read the appointment pages, or perhaps you might just skim them occasionally. And therefore anyone advertising in the recruitment classified section of a newspaper or magazine is only likely to be seen by people actively seeking a change of employment. So if your target(s) are happily employed and not job hunting, this method is a waste of money. The same is true to varying degrees for property, cars, travel and all other classified sections.

Okay, here's another example to emphasise this point. Many regional newspapers have commercial property classified sections. Now unless you're responsible for your own office building or retail premises when was the last time you read this particular part of your newspaper? Did you even know it existed? So if you are seeking to sell or let your office space and have identified that your likely targets are not looking for new premises at this time, you'll need to find another medium. Because of the way the print media, and newspapers in particular, are organised, classified ads all appear together in neat sections which are very easy for the reader to discard if they're not consciously, actively interested in that subject.

If you really know your target(s) and what they currently think and do, you'll work out pretty quickly if classified press advertising is for you or not. If it's not, then another option is run of paper. This is, as the name suggests, advertising which appears within the body of the newspaper. There are many options available to you including: choice of right- or left-hand page (right is more expensive); front or rear of the paper (the nearer the front the more expensive with front page being the most expensive of them all); facing editorial or not, etc. You can even specify which section of the paper your ad will appear in, sports pages for example, and of course there are choices of size of advertisement and whether it's to be black and white or colour.

When you consider that a broadsheet Sunday newspaper has more words within it than this book plus five others of equal size, you will begin to realise why so much advertising is waste. People often are misguided by the media sales teams with their impressive figures of how many thousands of readers they have and how these people all fit neatly into certain groups or classifications. At the end of the day, press advertising is often a hit or miss affair and the same ad running in the same newspaper on different days can have spectacularly different results.

The same can be said, by the way, for many other communications media also, not least direct marketing.

Example Redcup

Here is an example of a press advertisement Redcup has used to raise awareness amongst office workers (i.e. their secondary target audience).

How far do you have to go for great tasting coffee?

Get up from your desk.
Walk to landing.
Go down in the lift to the
   ground floor.
Leave the building.
Turn left.
Walk 200 yards in
   the rain.
Turn left.
Walk into café.
Queue for ten minutes.
Order a tall skinny latte.
Pay £1.75.
Wait for the bloke in the café to
   make your coffee.
Add sugar.
Stir.
Walk out of café.
Turn right.
Walk 200 yards (still raining).
Turn right.
Walk back into your building.
Wait for the lift.
Go back to your floor.
Walk back to your desk.

Get up from your desk, walk to the kitchen, place a proper china cup in the Redcup machine, press button marked latte, listen to the beans grinding, watch the fresh milk and espresso mixing, walk back to your desk, take the new business call, make the appointment.

Café quality coffee in your office

Tel: 020 8891 3148 www.redcup.uk.com

Client: Redcup
Agency: Phoenix

Direct marketing

I only did this as research for the book. Honest. I actually counted how many pieces of direct mail I received in one month. Have a guess. Wrong! 1,277. Staggering isn't it. And the variety ... possibly the most flattering was the opportunity to pay to go into space on a Russian rocket. At about $25million a go it's tempting, and yes I'd love to, but I'm not in that financial league ... yet! The most misdirected was from a company that manufactures bras for the larger woman (D cup and above only). Whilst I won't pretend not to have a healthy, and at times enthusiastic, interest in such matters, again, I'm not the right audience. Another surprising incentive was from an airline (no it wasn't BA), with special discounts which looked very tempting but actually expired the day before, as did an invitation to a charity concert – perhaps I should read something into this?

Of the 1,277, I responded to none. Not one of the 41 offers for a new credit card appealed, nor did the latest menus from the local Indian, Thai, Chinese and seventeen pizza delivery services. At work, I was offered new computers, corporate hospitality to every event imaginable and the chance to purchase special detection devices to spy on my colleagues and competitors! To name but a few.

Now I *have* been influenced by direct mail and this might account for my receiving so much of it, but the number of times is tiny compared with what I receive. Indeed, most specialist agencies will confirm that only around 1% of any mailing generates a response. Which means there's a huge amount of dead wood out there: literally. Whilst email doesn't have the same environmental effects, it's destroying many people's lives as spam proliferates at a rate at which rampant rabbits would be proud! I know of people who receive 200+ emails a day. Most of which they delete without even opening.

❝Possibly the most intrusive direct marketing is via the telephone❞

Possibly the most intrusive direct marketing is via the telephone. Every weekday, without exception, I get called by someone from a New York investment firm. They are the most persistent people I've ever encountered and despite every possible put down I can think of, they still come back for more. I now know how to beat them at their own game (that of wasting my precious time). I immediately ask, "Can you hold for a moment?" and they always reply "Yes," which gives me permission to put them on hold for as long as I like. I never go back to them but this does clog up my line for other calls. Direct marketing by telephone needs to be very carefully managed and implemented by trained professionals who really know what they're doing. I would advise extreme caution for most businesses before utilising this means of communication.

The point is this, direct marketing can be very effective when it's properly managed, which primarily means that people actively desire you to write/email/call them with news, etc. (for more on the subject read Seth Godin's excellent book *Permission Marketing*) but I suggest that at least 99% of direct communications employ the strategic thinking of pond life and motivate people to get upset and angry rather than to buy – and you don't want to do that, do you?

I like direct marketing very much and believe it can be very powerful and cost effective, but because it's so intrusive, I'd urge you to plan your campaign very carefully.

Example Redcup

Here are two examples of direct mail pieces that Redcup has used to target finance directors.

Client: Redcup
Agency: Phoenix

Client: Redcup
Agency: Phoenix

PR

Possibly the most misunderstood communications method is PR. Once again, its definition varies. I describe it in this context as the generation of information about your company, your products and services. Many companies only allocate a fraction of their overall budget to PR and yet it can be so powerful when compared with other media and often is far and away the most successful and cost effective.

Let's look at some of the downsides first. PR is not something that you can generate instantly, nor is it easily measurable, or controllable – its unpredictability scares a lot of people. However, it's the very fact that it isn't paid for advertising which makes it so powerful. Think about it, the overwhelming majority of "news" you watch, read or hear has a PR machine somewhere in the background. All government departments invest heavily in PR so their particular spin on events is portrayed. The same is true for other institutions, big business and the best small businesses too. So whether you're aware of it or not, PR is influencing you every day. And you can use it also to gain awareness of your business, in a way that no other medium can, as it appears in a more "believable" format than other communications.

There are many methods one can utilise to generate PR coverage and each has its place in your marketing tool kit. Far and away the most successful is to have someone within your company give PR the priority it deserves. If it's not top of someone's agenda it won't be effective, largely because it requires an instant response in many situations. This person doesn't necessarily have to be the chief executive although some of the best exponents of PR are (think Sir Richard Branson and Anita Roddick). Whoever you choose to be your spokesperson must be someone who can successfully communicate with journalists, someone who is instantly likeable and someone who will put themselves out to help a journalist get the story they want.

You have now completed HEMP steps four, five and six so you know which papers and magazines your targets read, which TV programmes and stations they watch and their favourite radio stations. With this in mind, you can create a media schedule and then, having completed HEMP steps seven and eight identify the messages you want to appear. Now it's all about how these can be packaged (or spun) so that a journalist will write about them. For example, let's imagine you've developed a new product which you believe will transform your industry. If it's truly revolutionary you might get away with issuing a press release or managing a press briefing to several key journalists. However, more often than not, this will not be sufficient to gain the attention you desire, so instead you need to think about how it can be packaged. One way is to use a real case study, another to tell a true story which just happens to include your innovation as the hero.

I honestly believe that there is a place for PR in just about every marketing campaign, for nearly every product and service. I don't believe this to be true of any other communication method, and ask you to add PR to your list of methods if you haven't done so yet.

A word of caution though – PR is not something you can totally control, in fact, it can get out of control in some cases. But these tend to be extreme cases and I suggest shouldn't put you off using PR within your HEMP.

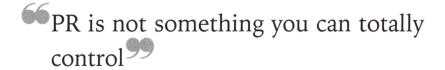

PR is not something you can totally control

Example Redcup

Redcup has generated significant PR coverage by using research and statistics on employee tea break routines and office drinks consumption to create newsworthy storylines.

Counting the cost of your daily cup

The price of your morning cappuccino may be higher than you think, according to a report released today.

EMPLOYEES popping out for a cup of coffee can cost employers the equivalent of up to £25 per head in lost time, according to office coffee machine company, Redcup.

Time spent away from the desk taking coffee breaks in trendy coffee shops results in vast amounts of lost revenue for companies, and effectively constitutes a 'skive' off work. The report continues to say

Client: Redcup
Agency: Phoenix

Sponsorship

Sponsorship is a real hit and miss affair for the most part, although there are some companies which use it to brilliant effect. Major, global brands know that the association with sports success is very powerful for them given its influence on their targets. Unfortunately they also share the negative effect of backing a loser. Take Vodaphone. Their sponsorship of the Australia Rugby Team, which had been unbeatable until the last World Cup, has resulted in masses of positive images of smiling heroes on TV, newspapers and magazines all with the Vodaphone logo very prominently in view. However, often in the same days, again on the TV and national newspapers, there are another group of sportsmen, too often looking desperate, upset and quite a sad bunch as they struggle to come to terms with yet another defeat, who also wear the Vodaphone logo, albeit that it's not looking quite so proud on the shirts of English cricketers. What do you read into these images? If you conclude that Vodaphone must be a successful company to be involved with Australian rugby then surely you'll take the opposite view about English cricket sponsorship? Or perhaps not. Maybe that British spirit of just being involved is all that matters. However, I'd imagine that when each sport comes to renegotiate its sponsorship deal then Vodaphone will treat each quite differently – wouldn't you?

In simple terms, I suggest you expect to get nothing back from sponsorship in terms of business generation and, if it's still worthwhile for you, then do it. Many small companies will sponsor school sport teams or local events, and this will create goodwill of course, but the commercial benefit for most is non-existent.

Example Redcup

Redcup agreed to sponsor a school football team. Despite attempts to justify this expenditure as having a marketing benefit, the reality is that a teacher at the kids school is married to one of the Redcup directors! Everyone was very happy though and the kids thought the kit was really cool!

Client: Redcup
Agency: Phoenix

Internet

Remember the story of the record company producer who told The Beatles that "guitar bands are finished" six months before they recorded "Please, Please Me" with EMI? Well, I recall a client saying in a meeting (in fact it's recorded in the minutes of a meeting held in July 1999, and we still pull it out for a laugh some days), that no-one will spend even 5% of their communications budget on the web! Whatever the fate of the majority of the 1990s dotcoms, the fact is that the web is the single most powerful new media since television, which some believe it's eclipsed. And if you don't include it within your communications strategy you clearly are a possible descendant of the Diplodocus!

"The web is the single most powerful new media since television"

Think of the web as a newspaper, radio station and TV channel all rolled into one, which every one of your targets visits regularly. But please get into the minds of your customers – what is it that they really want from your website? Do they really want to sit there for several minutes watching your "oh so clever" flash introduction? NO! Do they want to have to guess where they can get the information they want by pushing several buttons? NO! Do they want to visit every page as the only way of finding the small but relevant details? NO! So many companies seem to suffer a complete change of personality when it comes to their website, and often they end up looking like mutton dressed as lamb.

In addition to the look, content and navigation of your website you need to think about how you promote its existence. A general rule is to put the URL on everything, but I'm not convinced this is right. If you're seeking some other more direct response, such as a phone call or visit in person, then I'd seriously consider not always including it on your advertisement or direct mail piece. Which other websites would it be useful for yours to appear on as a link? People will click from one site to another to get more information so think about which sites you can contact with a reciprocal arrangement.

Possibly the most important thing to have in place is a clear proposition for your website visitors, i.e. what is it you want them to do next? State it clearly and boldly.

Example Redcup

Here are some pages from the Redcup website **www.redcup.uk.com**

Client: Redcup
Agency: Phoenix

Ambient media

Ambient media is a term used to describe every other media. Nowadays there's a plethora ranging from the tee markers on golf courses to toilet walls in motorway service stations. It seems that no surface is safe from advertising and, in the opinion of "Remote Viewer" Joseph McMoneagle, in his book *The Ultimate Time Machine,* the next big thing for advertisers is "billboards" projected into the sky! Be very careful with ambient media. The ideas always sound cool and different, and many are, but the response rate is extremely varied and as a rule of thumb, ambient should be used as a cautious bolt-on to a campaign.

Example Redcup

Redcup strategically placed these pavement stickers outside coffee bars which were frequently visited by office workers to make them stop and think before buying. A classic example of how ambient media can be an excellent means of creating intrigue and raising awareness through its use of unusual locations (in this case the pavement) to grab people's attention at the most appropriate moment (just as they are about to enter a coffee bar to purchase a more expensive coffee).

Client: Redcup
Agency: Phoenix

I know you already know a lot of this stuff. Hopefully you know a bit more now as you begin to select the best communications media for your business. In nearly every case I can think of it's a combination of media and creative devices and treatments which will achieve the optimum results. Very rarely indeed is one advertisement alone going to get the results you seek, or for that matter, one direct mail piece, one PR article or one anything. Of course, your choices will be substantially influenced by the amount you're prepared to invest and it's this part of HEMP that we'll look at now.

HEMP STEP 11 Key points

● There are lots of communication options available to you

● Understand what is and isn't possible from each type of communication medium

● Choose very carefully the most relevant and cost effective

HEMP in action   example 12

It's often the more glamorous products that make their advertising look good. Think about it, how hard is it to create an advertisement for a Ferrari? And yet there are many examples of outstanding creativity which have been used to make something quite dull appear interesting and worthy of your time to explore further. I've selected from many candidates this brilliant piece of art direction for the *Guardian* created by BMP DDB. Maybe it's just me, but I get a thrill from seeing great ideas and this is one with which I'd love to have been involved.

Client: The *Guardian*
Agency: BMP DDB
Art Director: Feargal Ballance
Copywriter: Dylan Harrison
Creative Directors: Jeremy Craigen and Joanna Wenley
As shown in the *D&AD Annual 2002*

HOW MUCH?

Clients will often say to their agency, as Managing Directors will also say to their marketing teams, "If I tell you the budget you'll spend it." My response is always the same, "That's right, so tell me how much you'd like to spend." I've never known a marketing budget not to get spent somewhere or somehow and I've seen many go over. Why muck about playing games? Either you're going to make the investment or you're not. Now before you go any further, remind yourself of how much money your desired result is going to make (see HEMP step two). And, unless you're a dotcom or have a very unusual business model I suggest that the starting point in determining your HEMP budget is a figure lower than both the turnover and profit you've identified! Now this doesn't mean you have to spend it all at once in the style of 1960s pools winner Viv "spend, spend, spend" Nicholson – indeed in a couple of steps time we'll look at measurement of your investment over time – but pick a figure. Come on, you have one already don't you?

The very best HEMP has a series of stages, which enables resources and the level of investment to increase, if necessary, in direct proportion to the results. Sometimes there needs to be a significantly higher upfront investment to get the early momentum and, on the face of it, your HEMP might not be progressed because the size of investment is just too large. If you're in this situation perhaps you could consider at this stage rethinking your strategy without having to abandon your desired result. For example, GMAC Residential Funding, a General Motors Company, opened for business in 1998. Although it is one of the largest lenders in the USA it had no business, reputation or brand in the UK. As its competition included former building societies, such as the Halifax, who have invested hundreds of millions of pounds over many decades, it was decided not to even try and compete in the same way. The idea of marketing GMAC Residential Funding to the consumer was scrapped; it was just too expensive even for a General Motors Company. Instead the selected tactic has been to promote the company, its products and services to financial advisors and encourage them to inform the ultimate customer of what's on offer. Despite investing less than 1% of what the major competition invest, GMAC Residential Funding is the UK's thirteenth largest mortgage lender overall and is number one in the highly competitive sub-prime mortgage sector. Often it's how creative you are with your strategy that will determine your success.

> **It's how creative you are with your strategy that will determine your success**

A question I'm often asked is, "What percentage of revenue should be invested in marketing?" To be honest I have no accurate answer, and nor does anyone else, indeed Lord Leverhulme, the English industrialist and philanthropist who set up Unilever, is believed to have said, "Half the money I spend on advertising is wasted, and the trouble is I don't know which half!" There are so many factors which will determine how much you will eventually need to spend it's impossible to predict accurately and it's this, more than anything else, which causes so many problems for marketers, and indeed why HEMP was created. Another common request is for a guaranteed return. "If I spend X can you at least guarantee that we will generate Y?" is something many marketing directors have been asked time and again. The only two answers, yes and no, are equally lacking in substantiation – it's really a leap of faith. And it's this, or your "gut reaction" if you prefer, that should be called upon here. Creating a HEMP will add considerable weight to your funding request, but at the end of the day it's how you feel, what you truly believe in, that will cause you to spend the money on communications or not.

It is extremely difficult to conduct marketing experiments in a controlled environment, because no-one is in control of their environment. Take your competitors – however much you'd like to, other than buying them, there is no way you can control them. Take your target audience – you now know more about them than you did before, but how are they feeling today? Or how will they react to next week's news? Your product might be exactly what they need for their business to soar into orbit, but will anyone notice if their offices burnt down last night, or even if something less dramatic occurred such as the Managing Director resigns or even if sales have dropped 25% in the last quarter? Possibly the most frustrating thing about marketing is that we can't know before we spend our money what the result will be. One thing though, with a HEMP you'll know much more than without one and will have eliminated many potentially wasteful practices along the way.

66We can't know before we spend our money what the result will be99

One of the reasons for the HEMP process having at the start a very specific desired result is the ability to focus on this alone and ensure that everything, including the investment required, is in alignment. Of course you can combine several HEMPs and discover that they can share many resources, including the communications budget, but I feel it's sensible to make sure that each element stacks up on its own merits. If you're not going to achieve the right return or if your investment is too high or too risky, then it might cause you to rethink things. And surely it's better to discover this now, during the planning stage, than after the launch and investment of a lot of money.

To conclude this step, and I accept that the lack of any exact formula or similar is frustrating, try this out: ask yourself "What is the absolute maximum I would spend on marketing and communicating to get this desired result of mine?" Then take three-quarters of this figure as your budget. It's about as scientific as any other method, you'll have a 25% reserve for contingencies (undisclosed) and, if you don't need it, well, your profit has just increased significantly.

Example Redcup

With limited start-up finance available, Redcup had just £75,000 to invest in marketing communications which needed to generate £1.3 million income within twelve months. This clearly had a direct influence on the communications strategy.

The Redcup directors determined the minimum figure they felt they needed to get their initial desired result (see step one). Subsequently they have invested considerably more, indeed it would not have been possible to create all the examples of different communications you've seen in this book for the initial budget. Their HEMP identified a sum of money they were prepared to lose if the venture didn't work out as planned. Fortunately the plan worked extremely well but it was useful to identify the "bail out" figure, and you might like to do so as well.

HEMP STEP 12 Key points

- Always have a marketing budget
- Set the budget in advance and expect to spend it
- Share your budget with key people and your agencies – don't play games

HEMP in action   **example 13**

I had to find a way to shoehorn this image into this book. The first time I saw it I just thought "Wow, I wonder how long it took to come up with that idea?" Then it struck me how incredibly clever to shoot it in this way, which looks so real – after all nurses are angels aren't they? In my opinion it's a work of art (and I don't care how pretentious that might sound), and I'm sure the RPA Foundation is extremely grateful to Lowe Hunt Lintas, the agency who created it.

It would have been easy to create a more obvious image, something which might have more initial standout, but this one lingers in the memory and has, in my opinion, much more likelihood of provoking a reaction. I urge you to use this as a benchmark, particularly when you've got a limited budget. A great image will work much harder and much more effectively than yet another obvious one.

Client: RPA Foundation
Agency: Lowe Hunt Lintas
Photographer: Gary Sheppard
Art Director: Adam Whitehead
Copywriter: Laurie Geddes
Creative Director: Lionel Hunt
As shown in the *D&AD Annual 2002*

OTHER RESOURCES

It's not just money you'll need to get your desired result. You need people, equipment, office and factory space, and so on: resources. And these should be, indeed I believe must be, identified before you start. In fact, your plan has a much greater chance of failure if you don't adequately identify and secure the necessary resources in advance. Fortunately, if you do then the opposite is true. Imagine climbing a mountain (a metaphor much quoted in business); you wouldn't wait until you got three-quarters of the way up it to discover you needed more rope, would you? It seems that many of us have some kind of pioneering spirit within us that causes us to believe we can take on any obstacle once we encounter it and the important thing is to make a start and get going. I can relate to this, and I'm sure you can too, but whilst it might make for an exciting marketing plan it will almost certainly be less than effective.

Of all the resources, the most important to gain advance commitment from, is people. You see, they have their plans too (often these are referred to as agendas, as in "What's his/her agenda?"), and whilst your desired result is utterly compelling for you it might be considerably less appealing to others, particularly if it means more work for them. Later we will look at some tips to get other people on board, enthusiastically, but as a start point it makes sense to share your ideas for the desired result as soon as possible, so that others feel involved and indeed can contribute. Help them to feel that this is their desired result too, not just yours. I suggest you look beyond the list of the 'usual suspects'. There might be several different people you work with who are itching to do something extra, who would jump at the chance to make a very positive impact. The issue is then how to find them? Word of mouth will normally do it – I've seen many people volunteer for things over a conversation at lunchtime or down the pub after work.

66Look beyond the list of the 'usual suspects' 99

Remember that it's not just the people you work with that can be your resources. Suppliers, not least agencies, are often prepared to invest time and effort in the beginning, in return for a commitment that they will get the business uncontested when it all kicks off. Of course anyone giving their time for free or at a significant discount is going to need to believe that your idea has legs, which of course is another reason for creating your HEMP. The additional benefit of external resources is that they only have one agenda – for your idea to work so that they, as well as you, benefit. This will often cause them to be very honest in their critique of your plan and this, even if it's painful, has the advantage of another perspective than your own. Two heads are more often than not better than one, so long as they're the right heads!

Many a plan has been killed off by accountants. As a breed they're averse to risk and whilst they tend to have an opinion on everything and can cite with considerable authority why things went wrong, their whole attitude to life tends to be spent staring in the rear view mirror with little attention given to what lies ahead. Unfortunately, your plan will need their support, particularly if it's competing with other plans for limited resources. In some accountants' hands those extra desk spaces, which currently sit there unfilled, immediately have an overhead cost should your plan occupy them. That redundant computer, share of the photocopier time and cost of the meeting rooms might get allocated to your project and yet these would still be borne by other current ventures were your plan to remain in the cupboard. You need to get these Spock-like creatures on board early. Get them excited. Cause them to see how an initial "rent and existing resource-free period" will pay back substantially in the longer term, with no downsides. Have them make your case for you. Indeed in many companies the magic words, "I've run this by (insert name of senior accountant or finance director) and he believes the numbers add up," are rarely improved on in the securing finance stages. You'll need resources to get your desired result. What are they? And if you don't know, please, please find out. If in doubt inflate them, as no-one likes surprises of the "Can I have more?" variety.

"Get these Spock-like creatures on board early"

Of course, you can go too far and attempt to predict things in the future which will actually harm your chances of making your HEMP come into action. It might be that in year seven you'll need 100,000 square metres of warehouse space, but that shouldn't occupy your mind, or one sentence of your HEMP if you're a start-up with no business at all yet. I suggest that for start-ups and smaller businesses the maximum time to project forward is three years and to be honest, for most, twelve months is more than enough. Indeed, very few businesses of any size can honestly say that their five-year plans ever come into reality, and as for those who plan twenty-five years ahead – all I can say is good luck!

Example Redcup

As a start-up business Redcup had limited resources and largely had to beg and borrow whatever it could. This included office space and facilities from a family member as well as the use of a car, etc. The Redcup team was extremely persuasive resulting in my agency giving them marketing services on a "pay us when you can" basis. The team of just two people quickly doubled, then doubled again, but the same approach has been adopted, only paying for resources when they absolutely have no other choice. As the chairman of Redcup has other business interests he was persuaded to commit half a day a week to the new business drive and a finance director from another company also promised to lend his assistance. Of course, there came a point when the company needed to stand on its own two feet and this was identified in terms of sales and gross profit targets before trading commenced. Fortunately, the team achieved this well within its defined timetable.

HEMP STEP 13 Key points

- It's not just money you need, other resources will be necessary to implement your plan – what are they

- It's important to identify all the resources you need up-front, before you start to put your plan into action

- Other resources, particularly people, will contribute more to your overall plan the earlier they are involved

HEMP in action example 14

Your product might be brilliant and the best in its field, yet so many people will select it or reject it based on their first impression, which may be unfairly based on the packaging. You can't judge a book by its cover yet people do. So when you've got the market-leading product and have established this as the preferred brand of choice across the world it would be very tempting not to make any radical changes. Heinz however has recently made a number of changes to that old staple, ketchup. There's been green and purple ketchup for example, but I like the way they've introduced positive messages onto the bottle labels. Something you might like to consider as your packaging represents an opportunity for self-promotion.

Client: H J Heinz Company
Design Group: Leo Burnett (Chicago)
Design Directors: Mike Straznickas and Dave Reger
Designers: Mike Straznickas and Kevin Butler
Copywriters: Dave Reger and Jim Bosilijevac
As shown in the *D&AD Annual 2002*

MEASURE IT

Tom Peters is credited with first saying "If you can't measure it, you can't manage it," and I believe this to be so true. Imagine a sprint athlete training without a stopwatch, or a top chef not having a thermostat on their oven. You wouldn't expect a school to award a scholarship without some form of test or examination and certainly no scientist could conceive of publishing a new theory without detailed analysis and measurement of results. And yet, when it comes to marketing, so many companies just don't bother to measure their results or in many cases, pay lip service to measurement. It's this which causes a vast amount of money to be wasted everyday. So will you waste yours or are you persuaded that you must have measurements in place?

Once you've accepted this principle the question you need to find the answer to is, "How will you measure your marketing investment?"

I once knew a businessman who was so exasperated by his marketing team's inability to accurately record, measure and analyse its expenditure he cut every single budget to zero to see what would happen. The marketing team screamed, the sales people went ballistic, the agency

❝He cut every single budget to zero to see what would happen❞

wasn't exactly thrilled but after a period of massive decline it caused everyone involved to think much more carefully about how and where they would spend the company's money and a 23% saving was the eventual outcome. This example is deliberately extreme, and many companies wouldn't survive such a radical action, but it caused people to stop and think about why, where and how the marketing investment should be made.

The most obvious measurement is sales, and to be fair, most do measure this. However, sales analysis can and should be very detailed with factors such as product line, territory, time period and individual performance all taken into account. Sales analysis on its own is not nearly enough and often gives results far too late. Consider the elements which must be in place to make up a sale. What is the percentage of enquiries which convert to buyers? How long do these take on average? What numbers of repeat sales do you achieve against new business? There are literally hundreds of different criteria, some of which will be highly relevant and appropriate for your business to measure.

Many years ago I worked in estate agency and my Chairman, Alan Robinson, developed a very simple model for predicting business levels which his highly successful business still uses today. Alan would work backwards starting with the annual turnover each office should generate. He would then work out exactly how many properties needed to be legally completed in the year and the timetable, taking into consideration the average selling price and average fee. From this the next step was to establish the ratio between the number of properties needed to be "listed" and the number sold. He also factored in the number of viewings per sale and the number of applicants (potential buyers), together with an average cancellation rate. From the measurement of these key criteria he could forecast to within a few percent exactly what each office would generate, and the problem cases stuck out a mile. Even this simple yet excellent system still didn't measure the marketing expenditure however.

What Alan's system didn't measure was how many enquiries and how much business came from the several millions invested in advertising, direct mail, PR and other communications. Indeed the view used to be, "Let's continue what we're doing if it's working." Very few business people in my experience have his natural instinctive intuition for what works and what doesn't and therefore I would suggest that for nearly all businesses measurements other than sales are required.

How you go about measuring will largely be determined by the type of business you have and the sector in which you operate. For many businesses it's very simple to have a dedicated phone line for sales enquiries and to measure the number of calls. Taking things further, enquirers should be asked which advertisement they've seen and are responding to. However, this is not always possible, indeed for some businesses it would be far too expensive and take too long to get this information. If this is your situation consider taking a sample of customers and finding out which of your initiatives they responded to. As long as your sample is large enough and is representative of all your customers it will give you a clear indication.

Possibly the easiest communication medium to measure is your website. Set up properly, you can see how many people have visited your site, how long they stayed, which pages they viewed, and for how long. The web is fantastic for gathering this type of information. Again though, many companies don't bother to analyse this data or fail to see the benefits they can gain from it. Let's imagine, for example, that you're offering different products to the same customers: would it be of interest to see how long a visitor to your website spends reviewing each product before adding it to their shopping basket? What if you discovered that on average 1:100 visitors bought product A and 1:500 bought product B. Might you do something about this? What if you were to offer an incentive to people to add a quick comment about your products? Would this feedback be useful for future development? The web provides marketing people with a brilliant feedback and measurement tool – only a tiny percentage of you are using it. One of my clients, Laing Homes, analyses its website very carefully indeed. "Deb the web" (Laing's webmaster) helped us come up with an ad campaign which was very effective. She noticed that 40% of all web visits occurred between noon and 2.00 p.m. on Monday lunchtimes. With hindsight this seemed obvious, people were reading the property sections of newspapers at the weekend and then on Monday at work, they would surf the web for more information. We ran the following ad in *The Sunday Times*.

❝The web provides a brilliant feedback and measurement tool❞

This just goes to prove how the right kind of measurement can help you to produce highly creative communications which are very relevant as well as having impact.

Some types of marketing communications are more difficult to measure than others. PR, for example, is regarded by many as extremely difficult, not least because of its unpredictability. This doesn't diminish its importance or effectiveness, so you need to find ways of making sure that your investment in PR can be measured. One of the most simple is to just ask clients, "Did you see the article in the xyz magazine?" Whilst not particularly scientific it will at least give you some feedback. With respect to PR, an essential requirement is to know the magazines, newspapers, websites and other media your targets regularly see. If you know the key messages that they are likely to respond to it doesn't take too much grey matter to work out that if you get these messages in the right places you'll get results. And yet, despite how blindingly obvious this is, so many people measure PR success by the amount of clippings they have accumulated, regardless almost of what these clippings are about or where they're from!

Other methods such as advertising and direct mail have the advantage of being tested in several ways and a sample can be measured prior to making the full investment. This is sensible to do for any major initiative as there are so many variables which can have an influence on a campaign's success. The timing of the mailing, the creative look, the headline message, the photograph or image – it's a long list. So if you're able to try out pilot mailings or advertisements and measure the different responses before committing to one execution I strongly recommend you do so. A word of warning though: an advertisement in a newspaper can generate wildly different levels of response in one week compared to another, as can two identical mailings. The reasons why can often be explained by the catch all "other factors" such as competitors' activity, or outside influences such as a major news story creating a different climate for your target audience. These factors are often used as excuses by people as to why they don't bother to accurately record their response to marketing, and in my opinion they're pretty lame. Over time these other factors will even themselves out of the equation or you'll be able to highlight them through exception reporting.

The methods which work for you today are not necessarily going to work so well next year, or maybe next month or even next week. One of the very few constants in life is change, and whilst people say they fear and dislike it, that's contradicted by the desire for new things which many of us seem to have. Therefore it's very important to continue to measure the response to your marketing initiatives so as to ensure you're continuing to get value for money. All too often companies continue to do the same thing and yet, in the face of declining enquiries and sales, are scared to change. Often this leads to greater expenditure as new ideas and media are eventually tried out in addition to the long-established methods. And, as you're reading this to make your marketing highly effective you wouldn't do that – would you?

❝One of the very few constants in life is change❞

Example Redcup

Redcup measures all enquiries via a dedicated phone line and asks everyone where they discovered Redcup. The Redcup website has a detailed reporting system and for special initiatives a dedicated, separate website has been used. As a lot of Redcup's business is generated through recommendation this is encouraged and monitored. Incentives are given for people who use Redcup to hand out referral literature to guests who compliment them on their coffee and this is also measured. For every direct mail campaign there's a special reference number to be quoted (or asked for) which also applies to the website, and this helps track the number of respondents.

In short, Redcup measures all its marketing activity and knows very quickly which initiatives are working well, identifying swiftly those which need adjusting.

HEMP STEP 14 Key points

- Measure your return on marketing by identifying up-front the things to measure

- Sometimes it's the less obvious indicators which are the most effective

- If you rely on sales figures or income alone your measurement might be too late to take action

HEMP in action   example 15

In communications, words and pictures should work together. If the words don't add something then, as a rule of thumb, leave them out. Here we can see two examples of how copy can make or destroy a great ad. So often it's tempting either to be too literal or to be so clever that the point is lost. Brilliant creative people, like those who created this ad for Nike, know the difference – do you?

It's not just what you say.

It's how you say it.

Client: AAA School of Advertising
Agency: The Jupiter Drawing Room (South Africa)
Product: Corporate
Creative Director: Graham Warsop
Art Director: Vanessa Pearson
Copywriter: Lawrence Seftel
Awards won: 1997 Cannes Gold (Print), 1997 New York Festivals Gold (Magazine), 1997 Eagles Silver (Print) – Eagles is a local awards festival in South Africa

WHAT NEXT?

I teach HEMP to many companies as an interactive workshop and it's at this stage that I normally say, "You're now ready to make a written commitment! Take a piece of paper and write down the next ten steps you will take and then prioritise them." For some this causes "planning panic" where they switch into corporate robot mode and start using language that they'd never dream of using at home or down the pub. Write *your* HEMP in *your* words. The actual act of writing your HEMP will create a far greater clarity and cause you to have many more insights than just leaving it in your mind. And the key to HEMP is to keep it simple, relevant and above all bullshit free! If you would like a HEMP template it's available in two versions, free of charge to download, from **www.phoenixplc.com/hemp**. You'll also find other reference materials, ideas and case studies to help you put in place a plan to get you that desired result you identified at the start of this book.

66 The key to HEMP is to keep it simple, relevant and above all bullshit free! 99

Example Redcup

The first actions Redcup identified for its HEMP were:

1 Acquire database of financial directors of south-east companies with more than fifty employees

2 Set up dedicated telephone line for response

3 Draw up list of previous contacts for private briefing

4 Recruit three people for the sales team and train them the Redcup way

5 Brief agency to create direct mail campaign

6 Brainstorm PR ideas and create PR plan

7 Progress website; in particular consider navigation requirements and preferences of target audience

8 Recruit engineers for machine installation and train them to have the Redcup attitude

9 Find warehouse facilities and office premises for the first twelve months

10 Create logo and identity to be applied to all marketing materials and stationery

HEMP STEP **15** Key points

- All plans need a start point

- It's useful to identify the first ten or so steps, particularly if the plan will take some time to implement

- You feel better about completing stages of a plan rather than waiting until it's completed – set out the stages

HEMP in action   example 16

This ad is framed on my office wall. I put it up the day I started in business and it's travelled with me ever since. I love the fact that there's no headline, no logo, no bold type – in fact, all the things you normally find in an ad aren't there – which for me is what makes it so brilliant. I reckon it could appear today with the latest Aston Martin as the hero. You can get some great ideas by looking back at old ads. This one appeared in the press forty years ago.

For you, a possession that reflects immaculate taste and rare discrimination. Of nearly two million British cars produced annually, Aston Martin account for just three a day. Each painstakingly hand-built by master-craftsmen . . . true devotees of the marque. The DB5 is the fastest regular 4-seater G.T. car in the world. Top speed exceeds 150 m.p.h. Stops from 100 m.p.h. in 6 seconds. Murmurs through traffic and arouses interest everywhere. Experience the ultimate in high-performance motoring — DB5 ASTON MARTIN.

Aston Martin built 4 litre light alloy engine, 282 b.h.p.; twin o.h.c.; 3 carburettors; micronic air filter; oilcooler; 5-speed gearbox; automatic transmission optional; power assisted discs; alloy body shell mounted on light tubular structure and carried on steel platform safety chassis; air conditioning optional.

Aston Martin Lagonda Ltd., Newport Pagnell, Bucks. Tel: Newport Pagnell 720. London Showrooms: 96/97 Piccadilly, W.1. Tel: GRO 7747

Client: Aston Martin

Making your HEMP come alive

I hate ideas that remain ideas. They must fly or die in my book. Better to have made a conscious decision not to proceed with an idea than to leave it in that part of the mind labelled "maybe one day" which sits next to its elder cousin "if only".

I've been told that as much as 80% of thought is recurring. If this is true it's hardly surprising we have such little genuine thinking time. Waking up in the middle of the night is the mind's way of trying to make itself heard above all the clutter, but is rarely helpful. Writing your HEMP will at least help you sleep better! Having done this, you can then get on with making it happen.

I strongly believe that the most powerful human resources are volunteers. I've seen the work of the International Childcare Trust in Sri Lanka, where volunteers work with some of the most deprived children in the world and I just marvel at their achievements – all of which are given for free. I don't believe that the same work ethic and consequent results would be achieved through any other way. And whilst suggesting to colleagues, suppliers and other resources that working on your HEMP for nothing will be good for the soul it's unlikely to get their commitment in the same way! So, instead, offer them something else – a chance to share in making your idea come alive and a share of the resulting glory. You'll be amazed how good people will feel to be asked to get involved if you do so in a genuine "I really want you on the team" sort of way.

"The most powerful human resources are volunteers"

My coach, Ed Percival of leadingworks.com, persuaded me to try out a new mantra "I will never get it all done" and this change of thinking has helped enormously. No-one will ever get it all done and despite the best efforts of a thousand time management techniques, completion remains as far away as ever. This is true for all the people you will need to help make your HEMP come into being. However by offering to share future success, and by painting a picture of your desired result in the most compelling manner, you'll find that people will make time for your HEMP – they and you can get this HEMP to materialise.

"Break your HEMP down into bite-sized chunks"

Break your HEMP down into bite-sized chunks. Sure, let them have a taste of the big picture, and then describe in fine detail exactly how stage one will look. The most daunting tasks seem reasonable when managed in this way. Ask a first-time marathon runner or triathlete how much better they feel to discover their first training session is six minutes on the treadmill. As you achieve each stage have an occasion – a night out, a bottle of wine or jumbo sized box of chocolates – whatever turns your team on. Please do this. Volunteers get de-motivated very quickly if you just keep asking for more with nothing going back.

If possible, have someone in charge of each part of your HEMP. Ideally not you – your role is to steer the whole thing. It can be tempting to put the most senior people in the driving seat but resist this. Instead consider who is most likely to ensure things get done – a good PA is often a lot more effective than a boss in delivering the result, making things happen on time.

Talking of time, have a specific date for every action. And expect dates to slip. After all, your HEMP will be in addition to everyone's day job.

When they do slip reschedule a new specific date. Exact dates rarely slip more than three times, I've found.

Remember WIIFM (What's In It For Me) – how will your HEMP benefit your team individually? If you don't know, please find out, as we all have different buttons that need pressing. And when you do you'll discover more about your band of helpers and they'll be even more committed to your HEMP. Imagine if the roles were reversed – would you be more motivated if your specific ambitions were being addressed?

There comes a point with most HEMPs where you've got to go public. People often delay this for fear of losing exclusivity, particularly if their idea is potentially easily copied. This often results in a stifling period of inaction. My experience is that any risk is more often than not outweighed by the advantages gained. Testing your idea will reveal refinements and improvements you're not able to anticipate at the confidential planning stage. For sure, you may attract several imitators, but better this than your idea being locked up in a filing cabinet!

If at first your HEMP doesn't succeed . . . many, if not most, plans hit hurdles. These can seem terminal at first, not least as you and others have bought into your idea so totally that when people don't get it, you just can't believe it. I'll spare you the usual platitudes and instead suggest you just get on with it. If your HEMP is good enough, and by using the process you know it is, then you'll find a way around it. This might mean you need to change some things, maybe even stuff you thought essential at the outset. If it gets your desired result though . . . .

"Properly celebrate when you achieve your desired result"

My next thought is a very un-British one! Properly celebrate when you achieve your desired result. Go on holiday, drink that £500 bottle of wine, buy the car, whatever. And have a party, dance like no-one else is watching, publicly thank people in the best Oscar style, lose your head. You have invested hundreds of hours to get your desired result, you deserve it. I'll look forward to receiving your invitation.

HEMP lessons

I'**ve worked with over 500 companies to date**, showing them the HEMP process and then with many, helped them to implement the plan and therefore I've seen the results. The following are a selection of examples to illustrate some of the more surprising insights gained.

Linley

Linley, the furniture makers in Pimlico Road, London, make the antiques of the future. The average value of its products is several thousand pounds. By using the HEMP process, Ruth Kennedy, managing director of Linley, and her colleagues realised that the more often they had the chance to talk with clients the more business they did. The hard part was finding new ways to create opportunities for dialogue. Although the first desired result was to sell more major pieces of furniture in twelve months the solution came from the decision to market small and significantly less expensive gifts. The Linley design team, headed up by Craig Allen, produced hundreds of items ranging from photo frames to candle holders, desk accessories to table lamps; all with the Linley attention to detail and exacting standard of manufacture. Clients loved them and visited the store and the website on a much more frequent basis than before which caused them to see the new major pieces of furniture Linley were working on, which in turn resulted in larger orders. In fact, one customer who visited the shop for a £12 door stop for her dining room left after placing an order for a new dining room table and chairs!

The lesson

Sometimes all you need to do in business is speak more often with your existing customers as opposed to having to find new ones all the time. The great thing about existing customers is that they know what to expect and you don't have to second guess their reaction.

The Grape Shop

There are ten wine merchants and off licences on the Northcote Road in London SW11. One of these, The Grape Shop, an independent, has created a point of difference which is very effective. Recognising that customers are often reluctant to try new wines they actually gave bottles away to regular clients on the basis that if they liked a wine they could then order a case at a special discount. Not only did this result in case sales increasing tenfold, it was also extremely effective in securing customer loyalty in a very competitive marketplace.

The lesson

Sometimes clients need to sample something before they will buy it – that's understandable. Think up ways your prospects can have a relatively inexpensive and highly effective taste of things to come.

Robinson Low Francis (RLF)

Steve Barker, the senior partner of Robinson Low Francis (RLF), quantity surveyors and construction consultants with six offices around the UK, is not what you expect from a surveyor. He's funny, likes a good laugh and genuinely plays and works hard. Perhaps that's why his business is so successful. Indeed, here's another example of where personal relationships are the single most likely reason for winning business. RLF know its target audience very well indeed: 95% are male, aged

35–55, who are themselves professionals. Marketing to this group should be relatively easy, but how to do so in a memorable, different and motivating way is the challenge Steve set with his HEMP.

RLF entertains a lot and this is a key way of building relationships which in turn leads to more business. The thing is, most of its targets have been dined at Wimbledon, Twickenham, Goodwood, Epsom, Covent Garden – you name it, they've done it. So what could RLF do differently? Last year the Science Museum held an exhibition of James Bond memorabilia. RLF hired the venue exclusively and invited all its key audience to spend an evening surrounded by "Bond Girls" whilst sipping Martinis (shaken not stirred), and getting fitted out by Q with an Aston Martin of their choice! A near 100% turn-out and a subsequent 25% year-on-year increase in business just proves how effective communications are when you get them right at the emotional level. Think about it, do you know any male over 30 who isn't mad for James Bond?

The lesson

It's not always necessary to change a winning formula – entertainment works for RLF and other professional businesses. The key is to do something brilliantly well and differently, giving a true one-off experience. Incidentally, the investment, as in this case, doesn't have to be any greater than usual either.

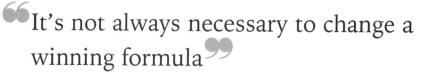

"It's not always necessary to change a winning formula"

Admiral Homes

David Holliday was Chief Executive of Admiral Homes, a major house builder in the south of England. David has been in the industry all his life and knows more than most about his industry, so much so in fact that his desired result was to find a way to stand out from the crowd – he recognised that there wasn't a lot to differentiate one builder from another. In creating his HEMP, David asked himself, "What is something you would never hear anyone say about a house builder?" And concluded that the answer lay in something he was seriously interested in – the environment. David's company pioneered energy-efficient homes and won numerous awards; in fact David himself received the OBE for his contribution. David will be the first to acknowledge that none of his companies are the largest house builders and yet by creating a point of difference received a level of publicity totally disproportionate to market share. Also, private and public landowners alike genuinely prefer doing business with a developer with a social and environmental conscience – the public love it too.

The lesson

In a competitive market place where several companies offer largely the same product and service what can you do differently? Having a significant point of difference creates many advantages, allowing you to stand out from the crowd.

Stackhouse Poland

Jeremy Cary has worked in the insurance business since he was eighteen. Despite this, he's a very interesting guy with bags of enthusiasm! After successfully completing a buy-out of Stackhouse Poland, insurance brokers, Jeremy and his partners turned their attention to how they could significantly generate additional new business in the first twelve months. The company's clients largely fall into two categories – corporate and wealthy private individuals. Amazing as this might seem, the previous owners hadn't made the observation that senior people within major corporate companies often tend to be privately wealthy. The HEMP helped show how if you could do someone a personal favour, such as significantly reducing their personal insurance premiums with no loss of cover, indeed in many cases with extra benefits, it became a very easy "sell" to ask, "Now can I look at your business insurance arrangements." A 52% increase in business has been the consequence of this very straightforward and simple approach.

The lesson

If you can benefit an individual personally then you're much more likely to gain their interest and the opportunity to sell them something else of more significance. By understanding that everyone in insurance claims to offer the best rates, best service, etc. Stackhouse Poland realised that it needed to find a way to prove that it really could. Focusing on individuals, most of whom were recommended by existing clients, it built a highly personal relationship, indeed often visiting the new clients at home to discuss their needs in greater detail. The relationship-building exercise then led to the bigger opportunities.

"The relationship-building exercise then led to the bigger opportunities"

Island Cruises

Island Cruises are, funnily enough, in the cruise industry. Or at least that's what we thought when we first met the company and saw its huge ship, the Island Escape. However, following putting a HEMP together to create more customers we all had a significant shift in thinking. Island Cruises is actually in the holiday business and it's competing with all the other package holidays on offer. This new direction resulted in a total rethink about the size of the market, the competition, in fact just about everything. The first step was to conduct research to find out exactly why customers chose their holidays and this confirmed the feeling that people wanted something different to the static, two weeks in one resort, yet at the same time liked the consistency of restaurants, bars and night life. The marketing campaign has a new focus to persuade people to try a different holiday in several resorts without having to pack and unpack several times, as opposed to focusing on cruise converts who already knew the benefits.

The lesson

Sometimes companies can become very focused on their business and sector and might not realise the huge additional potential that they don't need to create – it's already there. The extensive research exercise not only confirmed this gut reaction but also pointed out and highlighted the key motivation for customers, their concerns and desires. As a consequence an aggressive growth plan is being pursued.

Intrepid Travel

Intrepid Travel doesn't do holidays – it creates adventures for travellers. This company was founded by people who were bored of holidays, even those to the most far-flung destinations, as they found them so sterile and predictable – let's face it, one hotel with air-con and mini bar and twenty-four-hour room service looks much like another. So Intrepid promises its clients unpredictability, for example this is an extract from their brochure about travel arrangements, "At Intrepid we use a huge variety of local transport that becomes a highlight of the trip rather than just a means of getting from A to B. While we do use conventional trains, planes and automobiles we also use the non-conventional local buses, riverboats and bicycles. We also use the downright unconventional bemos, songthaews, cyclos, rafthouses or elephants – and let us not forget our feet!"

As opposed to the conventional star rating system (where five star is regarded as luxurious), Intrepid has an elephant rating – one elephant suggests a moderate level of comfort but check out this description for a five elephant trip, "You're out there in Asia and the Middle East. You are likely to be exposed to the elements and/or altitude, stay in very basic lodgings for extended periods, travel in whatever means of transport is available and basically take it as it comes, whatever comes! It can be tough."

The team at Intrepid realised that its own holiday requirements were just not being catered for and this was true for hundreds of others for whom it could provide a service. The team spotted a gap in the market based on its own experience. Today, Intrepid has two hundred people working for the company, offers over two hundred different trips to over thirty destinations. Visit www.intrepidtravel.com for more information on this very different and very successful company.

The lesson

Find the gaps. You may think that everything has been done before and yet it hasn't – new businesses start up every day with something different to offer. Whilst you are rarely your target audience, if you're in a start-up and without an idea that grabs you immediately, finding something you want could be the solution others are also seeking. Plus you find an answer to your own needs at the same time!

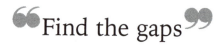
66Find the gaps99

Letterstone Investments

Simon Hill has run several successful businesses even though he was sacked after just one day from his first job as a waiter! His most recent venture, Letterstone Investments, buys large numbers of new flats from developers at a substantial discount which he then passes on as individual units to Letterstone's network of investors at the same discounted price, charging a small fee. The developer gets a volume sale, the investor gets to buy at a price they could never negotiate individually, and Letterstone makes money too – what I call a win, win, win situation!

The thing that separates Letterstone came when we created a HEMP together. Realising that investment is all about confidence, it was decided that not only would Letterstone make available to its investor database all the extensive background research that is carried out for every purchase; in addition Letterstone would put its money where its mouth is and keep at least one of the flats for the company. This effectively is saying, "look, this is so good we're investing ourselves for the longer term too."

The lesson

In the current financial climate, where there is so little confidence and so much suspicion, Letterstone has turned this on its head through leading by example – we're going to share the risk with you. Confidence is something all customers need – can you prove that your product or service is so good that you use it yourself?

Phoenix

My company, Phoenix, uses the HEMP process for itself. Recently we carried out a review of all our clients and noticed something that we'd previously missed. Although we're probably the largest and most successful marketing agency in Surrey, we had only one client in this county! We'd never thought about it before, but discovered there are hundreds of local businesses, of all sizes, to whom we could provide with marketing services. We'd previously been so focused on one business sector or another that we'd never thought about categorising clients by geographical location, and yet how much more convenient for everyone to have clients within a ten-minute drive away rather than across the UK? The consequent communications initiative (a mix of direct mail and PR) resulted in five new business wins in just three months, as we discovered that local businesses were fed up with paying London prices, not to mention the travel time and congestion charge on top of the extortionate parking! As most of us have worked for London agencies, we were able to offer "London on your doorstep".

The lesson

I thought I should show you how we take our own medicine and how we're still learning too. By looking at our clients from a different perspective we discovered in excess of 5,000 potential new business opportunities! Not bad from a one-hour planning session!

HEMP – final thoughts

I hope that the HEMP process, the Redcup case study, HEMP in action and HEMP lessons have inspired you to go for that idea of yours and to make it happen. I had no idea when we created HEMP as a process to help us understand clients' businesses better that one day I'd be writing about it and conducting regular workshops, but, of course, I hadn't produced a HEMP for HEMP then! (I have since, and hence written this book, amongst other things.)

Creating a HEMP will, more often than not, reveal many things about your business and indeed about you personally. I know people who have used the HEMP process to find another job; someone else used it to find a new home and to negotiate a better price; one guy I met said he used it successfully to find a new girlfriend! And if you stop and think about it, that's not really surprising as, after all, everything in life is marketed and sold.

❝Everything in life is marketed and sold❞

I know that a lot of the HEMP process is simple, obvious and most people know it already. The thing is, it might be common sense but it's uncommon practice, as illustrated by the millions of pounds that will be wasted today alone on ineffective marketing.

If you need further resources you can visit **www.phoenixplc.com/hemp** or send me an email to **hemp@phoenixplc.com**

Good luck and above all else please enjoy the highs that your HEMP will give you!

Postscript: how is Redcup doing?

My publishers thought you would be interested to learn how Redcup is doing and I'm delighted to answer this question with just two words – VERY WELL.

In the first year Redcup exceeded its sales and profit targets by over 50% and is set to repeat this in its second year. It has added several different machines to the Redcup collection which means that more companies of different sizes can get the benefit of "Starbucks in their office".

Plans for next year include machines which allow both decaffeinated and regular beans to be utilised at the same time (although not in the same cup!), desktop machines and machines which supply other fresh beverages including tea and hot chocolate.

Possibly the biggest lesson for Redcup, following its HEMP, is how people actually become quite emotionally attached to its products and service. Indeed reliability and speed of service are much more important factors than the directors had previously realised and they play on this when marketing the company against competitors. Yes, people want the finest coffee, but they want it within 30 seconds of arriving at their offices, and do not want to wait for the machine to start up or be restocked or even repaired. As a consequence, a major feature of the Redcup offer is its service, and clients can choose for their machines to be stocked and serviced every day, before they start work.

> ❝A projected turnover in excess of several million pounds within three years❞

Redcup uses HEMP every time it is targeting a new market or customer and finds the process as effective in helping it to close a one-off deal as it has been in launching the company from nowhere to a projected turnover in excess of several million pounds within three years.